Precious Children of INDIA

Giving Voice to Destitute Children of the World

Elizabeth A. Carpenter
Photography by Bruce M. Carpenter

Cover Images: Bruce Carpenter, ayakumar/Shutterstock

Cover Design: Amber Burger

Editor: Nancy L. Graves

Visit Elizabeth's website: www.hispreciouschildren.org

Precious Children of India – Elizabeth Ann Carpenter

RELIGION / Christian Ministry / Children

Printed in the United States of America

First edition published 2014

www.lifesentencepublishing.com

LIFE SENTENCE Publishing books are available at discounted prices for ministries and other outreach.

Find out more by contacting us at info@lspbooks.com

LIFE SENTENCE Publishing, and its logo are trademarks of

LIFE SENTENCE Publishing, LLC
P.O. Box 652
Abbotsford, WI 54405

Paperback ISBN: 978-1-62245-201-9

Ebook ISBN: 978-1-62245-202-6

10 9 8 7 6 5 4 3 2 1

This book is available from www.amazon.com, Barnes & Noble, and your local bookstore.

Share this book on Facebook:

Precious Children of INDIA

Precious Children
of
Kenya
Elizabeth A. Carpenter

About the Cover

We were walking through the slum that one of the children in this book, Kala, used to live in. A man asked if Bruce would like to take his daughter's picture. Bruce crouched down to see her inside this shanty in the slum. He saw this beautiful little girl just sitting there. Bruce went to take her picture and he shared that she was looking straight past him not even acknowledging that he was there. She did not smile or even react to his presence. She showed absolutely no emotion. She was like a little adult just sitting there who had succumbed to her situation, as if in her mind, this is all she has ever known, all that she does know, and all she will ever know. We later found out this little girl is Kala's cousin.

This book is dedicated to our Savior and Deliverer, Jesus, and to the precious children of India.

For He will deliver the needy who cry out, the afflicted who have no one to help.
He will take pity on the weak and the needy and save the needy from death.
He will rescue them from oppression and violence, for precious is their blood in his sight.
(Psalm 72:12-14 NIV)

Contents

Preface

Destination India

While walking through the exhibition hall at the International Conference on Missions, wondering where God would send us next to work with His precious children, Bruce and I were invited to have a seat at a booth featuring India. Here we met John from Life Light. He pulled out two chairs for us and asked about our church, and how we were enjoying the conference. He gave me a brochure and a calendar to look at as he explained the children's home that Life Light runs in India. While he talked, I looked at the pictures of the children in the calendar. One little girl, in the middle of a picture of girls, jumped off the page at me and I asked, "John, what is this little girl's story?"

He shared that this young lady smiling in the picture, and surrounded by her friends, had a very sad story. What he told us stirred our emotions to the point where we felt we had to take action. We left John telling him we would be praying for her.

As the day wore on, she stayed on our hearts. We left the conference and returned home, praying to God for His will on our next story-sharing mission trip, and if India was where He desired for us to go. When this story remained on our hearts, we decided to reach out to Life Light to see if they would be interested in working with us. The team at Life Light prayerfully considered our request and thought we should come to India to learn about the lives of these children.

We have been on mission trips to Haiti, Kenya, St. Vincent, and many within the United States. This would be our first trip to a restricted and unreached nation. Looking back, it is hard to describe the differences between unreached India and the Christian countries we worked in with people just as poor and destitute, although not as great in number, but I will attempt it. The people in the Christian nations had hope and joy in the midst of extreme suffering. For example, a starving woman in Kenya told us she had faith that God would provide, and showed us a small pile of nuts that would feed her family for the day. She had a light in her eyes and hope found in Jesus Christ. However, that same hope could not be found in the people in India. We did see it in the Life Light staff, but to the greater population of poor in India the hope found in Jesus was missing, making the situation seem more hopeless and destitute.

In preparation for the trip, we studied many materials on India and its culture. We learned from the Joshua Project's[1] study on Unreached People Groups that India's primary religion is

1 http://joshuaproject.net/

Hinduism, with 80.6 percent of the people groups practicing. We also learned that only 2.2 percent of the population is considered Christian.

India has a population of over 1.2 billion people with one third of the world's poor living there, or an estimated 269 million below poverty level, with another 414 million considered vulnerable.[2] Human trafficking is rampant, with an estimated 100 million people in bondage.[3] Although the caste system is considered illegal, from our observation, it is still very active in the lives of the people we talked with across the country. People get their education, job, and marriage partners based on where they fall in the caste system. Female feticide is rampant, with a baby girl being aborted, or killed at birth, every twelve seconds, an estimated 7,000 girls a day.[4] Women are burned to death over dowry issues by their spouses or their spouse's families. The list continues and the numbers are staggering just due to the massive population in India.

One year later, after our initial meeting at Life Light, armed by God and with all we had learned, we boarded a plane for India. The plan was for us to meet and travel with John's wife, Heather, a Life Light missionary. We would meet her in Chicago where the three of us would all travel to India together, then, we would meet up with John who was already over in India. Due to a storm, all of our flights were cancelled, so we quickly rerouted. We flew through Germany to Mumbai, while Heather flew another route. As a result, we were without

---

2 Dhawan, Himanshi. "India is home to world's 1/3rd of extreme poor population: UN study" *The Times of India*, July 17, 2014: http://timesofindia.indiatimes.com/india/India-is-home-to-worlds-1/3rd-of-extreme-poor-population-UN-study/articleshow/38512305.cms

3 "Official: More than 1 million child prostitutes in India" *CNN* May 11, 2009: http://www.cnn.com/2009/WORLD/asiapcf/05/11/india.prostitution.children/index.html?iref=24hours

4 Thomas, George "Disappearing Daughters: India's Female Feticide" *CBN News* Friday, July 06, 2012: http://www.cbn.com/cbnnews/world/2012/June/Disappearing-Daughters-Indias-Female-Feticide/

Heather's traveling experience. When our plane landed, we said a quick prayer thanking God for travel mercies and asked not to encounter any issues in customs with the bags of toys we brought for the children. The toys are critical to our mission's success. We use them to help interact and build relationships with the children we meet.

From our studies about India, we knew that the airport in Mumbai is next to one of the biggest slums in the world. The haze from the slum fires hung heavy in the air and the smell of human waste struck us immediately as we exited to the tarmac. However, we did not have time to focus on this because we were pushed forward by the crowd into buses that took us to the baggage claim area. Once there, we gathered our things but had trouble getting luggage carts. Every time the empty luggage carts came, there was a rush of people and they were grabbed up before we could get one. Some people were paying staff to go past customs and bring back a cart for them. We were just about agreed on how much we should offer, when a delivery of luggage carts was brought right next to us. We secured a cart for all the bags we brought, thankfully, because most of the other travelers had already gotten carts of their own.

With luggage on carts, and carts in hand, we joined our next line for bag inspection. We quickly learned that people in India get excited and push in line. It is not meant to be rude, it simply means they are excited, or so the man that kept pushing us along explained to us. We had practiced what we were going to say to customs (as close to the truth as we could), that the toys were gifts for the children our friends, who were teachers at an English school in India, worked with. Never once were we asked about our large duffel bags of toys, nor why we were in the country.

We made it through customs and then onto another bus. This bus took us to the area in the airport where we would meet

Heather for the final leg of our trip. We were grateful that the man who kept pushing us through the first line actually ended up in the line for this bus, too. He helped us get our things loaded onto the bus without expecting payment for the assistance, and he told us what we needed to do. Since Heather was not with us to speak Hindi, his ability to speak fluent English was very helpful. After a long exhaustive trip, we were truly thankful God sent someone who could help us the way he did.

Finally, we got to the hangar for flights within India and there was Heather waiting for us. By now, we were on sensory overload from taking in all the smells of the slum and new spices, as well as the sight of exotic colors in the beautiful clothes the women were wearing. India is a very beautiful country with a bounty of colors and flavors that we had just scratched the surface of at the airport.

We boarded a small plane and headed to our first destination to work with Life Light at New Beginnings Children's Home. When we arrived, John and his father, Papa, met us and gave us leis of flowers. We had a hearty breakfast at a local hotel and then headed to the children's home.

Bruce, Liz, Heather, and John arriving at our first destination in India

Normal mid-afternoon traffic as we travel to the children's home where we lived while in India

On the way to the children's home, we passed through a city and a village. Cows wandered the streets. Pockets of poverty, and luxury, were seen everywhere we looked with beggars and rag pickers sprinkled throughout.

India reported in their 2013 census that 65 million people lived in slums. The census defined a slum as "residential areas where dwellings are unfit for human habitation because they are dilapidated, cramped, poorly ventilated, and unclean or any combination of these factors which are detrimental to safety and health."[5]

Slums seemed to pop up in every open space, under bridges and in-between buildings. In the small towns and villages, the slums were out in the open. In the large cities, they were hidden behind walls. Through the open spaces in the walls, you could see they were there, just hidden from open view.

Mostly women, but some men, knocked on our car windows

5 Rukmini, S. "65 million people live in slums in India, says census data" *The Hindu* New Delhi, 1 October 2013: http://www.thehindu.com/todays-paper/tp-national/tp-newdelhi/65-million-people-live-in-slums-in-india-says-census-data/article5188234.ece

begging for money. Whenever we stopped, children came begging at our car too, surrounding us when we exited in the towns and city. Children walked through traffic selling various things, while others performed dances or gymnastics on the side of the road for the vehicles stopped at the lights, hoping people would throw them money.

In other areas, there were children hurrying to school in their uniforms, carrying their lunch buckets. Vendors sold bags of milk and water for the children to buy for school.

Bathrooms were a bit of a challenge. We frequently saw men urinating on walls or in the fields we passed through. We got used to the fact that we would see this everywhere we went in India. It was just as common in the towns as it was in the rural areas.

Driving in India was an experience in itself. Cars and motor bikes would weave in and out of lanes. Honking horns is a way to signal, so horns were constantly blowing. Cars went the wrong way down roads to get where they were going, whether there was room or not. We held on tight while trying to take in all the sights, and prayed for our safe arrival.

Once we arrived at the home, we were greeted by the children who were very excited to see us. The staff prepared chai and cookies for us to enjoy after our long drive. They gifted us with more leis and tons of hugs. Also, there were pictures to pose for to remember the occasion.

Something interesting we did not discover in our studies was that people in India love to pose for pictures. Every event we attended, or group of people we worked with, wanted to formally pose for pictures. So, after pictures were taken, we were ready to begin working with these wonderful, precious children in India.

Wild monkeys playing

Wild parrot nesting in a tree

Lady working in field

Families traveling on motor bikes is a common mode of transportation in India

Acknowledgments

First, and foremost, we thank God for the privilege of going to India to work with His precious children. This was a difficult trip for us due to the harshness of the children's stories. As we left each area we visited, we kept saying surely this is an isolated case. In each city, we read the newspapers, and over, and over again, the headlines mimicked the children's stories shared with us. We saw the slums, rag pickers, prostitutes, and child-laborers in brickyards and farm fields everywhere we travelled. We could not deny this firsthand experience or the hopelessness many children face in this country.

We want to thank our family, friends, and church family for giving us so much love and support as we prepared for, and travelled to and from this story-gathering mission trip.

Also, the missionaries with whom we now feel like family – the Life Light and New Beginnings Children's Home staff, Papa, John, and Heather.

We could not have done this project without the prayers and support of our Board Members – Dave, Theresa, Naomi, Kathy, and Bonnie; and of course, our supporters who gave so generously to support us on this mission.

We thank and send our love to all the precious children of India who were brave enough to share the good and the bad in their stories with us. Your strength, courage, dreams, and faith during difficult situations is truly humbling, and an inspiration to us.

Finally, we thank you for reading about the experiences of these precious children and for listening to their voice.

In His Service,
Elizabeth & Bruce

Introduction

This book is a compilation of first-hand interviews, file documentation, and cultural research. Each chapter contains the real life story of the individual child, incrementally by age and experience. The child is sharing their story with you just as they shared it with us. Due to India being a sensitive nation we had to protect the identities of the missionaries and children. Their names have been changed where required in order to protect them.

Also, there are many cultural terms used by the children in their stories which are defined below for quick reference:

Castes: Brahmin – Priests; Kshatriya – Warriors; Viasya – Merchants/Landowners; Shudra/Sudra – Peasants/Servants; Dalit – Untouchables

Ceremonies/Celebrations: Funeral Fire/Pyre – A form of cremation where the body is burned on a wooden platform; Mattu Pongal – Celebration of thanks for cows/oxen (Occurs on the third day of the four day long Pongal Festival)

Foods: Chai – Tea; Chapati – Unleavened flatbread; Chapati Upma – Breakfast dish made with Chapati; Dahl – Spicy lentils

Games: Carrom – A billiards-like game; Kho kho – A tag-like game

Relatives: Aaie – Mother; Aunty – Aunt; Baba – Father; Nana – Grandfather; Nani – Grandmother

Misc.: Babool Tree – Thorny-branched Acacia bush; Saree – A colorful Indian dress; Standard (in school) – Grade in school

Fruit and vegetable stands line the streets

Crowded shopping alleyways

Sikh Temple

Hindu shrine to the orange rock god

Diya

Age Four

I was very busy today. I helped Aaie take care of my younger brother, two-year-old Ashok. I played pots and pans while he watched, and helped play cook. My older brothers, Arjun, nine, and Santosh, six, played with us for a while too after school. We have plenty of food in our home. I live with my brothers, Baba, Aaie, Aunty, Nana, and Nani. Nana and Nani are Baba's parents. We've always lived with them in our apartment in the city. Baba and Nana are construction workers. Aaie and Nani take care of the home and the children. Aaie and Aunty do all the cooking. At night we always have a nice dinner. Nana and Baba are served first, then Nani, my brothers, and me. Aaie and Aunty usually eat when everyone else is done in the kitchen.

Ashok and I watch every day for our brothers to come home

from school. We also watch for Baba and Nana. Baba and Nana don't pay much attention to us. Aaie and Aunty play with me, but never Baba and Nana. I love to make my Aaie laugh when we play, she has a beautiful laugh. Nani tells us stories and helps Aaie with some of the housework. Sometimes, Nani beats Aaie when she upsets her. Nani scares me, so I always listen and do what she asks. Nani is in charge of the household and makes sure everything gets done. Aaie never talks back to Nani and always tries to please her. Baba and Nana work all day at the construction sites, then after dinner they leave to go play cards. Sometimes, Baba comes home in bad shape from alcohol. Baba has seizures sometimes too. It scares me when I see this happen to Baba. Aaie wants Baba to see a doctor but he doesn't want to spend the money, so he tells her he's fine.

Aunty is getting married in two days. She's only met the man she's going to marry one time. He is twenty-six and she is sixteen. He's a construction worker in the same caste as us, Shudras. There is a lot to do for the wedding, and Aaie is tired from all the extra work. Aunty's new saree is beautiful. There will be a big wedding celebration and the entire family will come. I'll get to see my cousins and there will be lots of good food. I'm excited about the wedding, but will miss Aunty living with us, because she'll go to live with her husband's family.

Tomorrow, early, we'll go with Baba to market. I like going to market and seeing all the food and other things to buy. My three brothers and I share a room. We wash up for bed, then go to sleep in our beds on the floor. Aaie and Baba have their own room. Nana and Nani also have their own room. Aunty sleeps in her own area. Our apartment is nice for us, and I'm glad we live here with room for everyone. We have a main room where we eat, worship, and play. We worship Hindu gods. Nani likes to worship the god Shiva. We have a picture of Shiva where we burn incense, and leave flowers and food as offerings. We pray to Shiva to help us.

We get up early and have chapati upma for breakfast. It is made with the left over chapati from last night. We also have milk and Baba has chai. Then, Ashok and I get ready to go to market with Baba and Aaie. I'm very excited to go to market. The market is crowded, with many smells and sounds. There are stalls selling spices, fruit, chickens, lamb, vegetables, and cloth. Also, vendors cook food to sell. Cows wander along the street looking for food. Children go through the trash with large white bags slung over their shoulders. They are called rag pickers and beg for food. I'm glad I don't have to live like these children.

As we shop, Aaie and Baba talk, when suddenly, Baba's words start to slur and he hits the ground. He is having a very bad seizure. Aaie screams for help for Baba. He keeps shaking and shaking, and his head is bouncing around, then it stops. People stand around us as Aaie calls for Baba to talk to her, but he's not moving. Baba is dead.

When we get home, Aaie cries out that Baba had a bad seizure and died. Nana and Nani are very upset as Aaie explains what happened. Nani gets up and yells at Aaie, "My son, my son you have poisoned and killed my son!" She starts beating Aaie, and yells, "Get out murderer of my son – your children are no longer living here!" Aaie begs Nani to listen to her that she did not kill Baba. Nani doesn't listen to her. Aaie, Arjun, Santosh, Ashok, and I all leave. At first, we turn to neighbors and Baba's other family members for help. But, no one will help us because Nani spreads rumors that Aaie killed Baba.

It's getting late in the day as we walk to a nearby bridge. Aaie tells us we'll stay under the bridge for the night. We have none of the things from our home except the clothes we had on our backs when we left. We lay on the concrete all huddled together, scared, hungry, and tired. I hear Aaie crying. The next day we scrounge for food and talk to other people living under the bridge. We learn of a place that gives money and bags to people so they can be rag pickers. We will pay them back through collecting scraps. We talk to a man there and get four large white bags. The bags are bigger than me. He gives us enough money for Aaie to get us some food, supplies, and a blanket to share. We build a fire and eat. We drink water from the stream. Next, we find enough cardboard for each of us to sleep on – but I cannot sleep. I have a very bad nightmare and see Baba dying, again and again. I wake up very scared with my heart racing, but I try to sleep some more.

Early the next morning we get up and Aaie walks with us to pick the trash. We work very hard looking through garbage piles and dumpsters trying to find plastic, newspapers, glass bottles, and metal. We also have Santosh gathering sticks for a fire. We beg for food from people who watch us from their homes, but no one helps. We find some food in the trash and eat it. At mid-day we stop to rest for a while. We're all very tired and Ashok falls asleep. We keep picking through the trash until late at night, and finally we've filled all four bags. We can hardly move them. We take them back to the man who has the money and sort out the glass, metal, plastic, and paper. He weighs what we've gathered and keeps what we owe him, then gives Aaie some money for us to use. I'm so hungry and tired, and I feel dirty. Aaie has us wash in the stream while she gets us some food. I hope Aaie will laugh and play with us like she used to before Baba died.

Age Six

I did not like living under the bridge and am happy that we do not live there anymore. We now live in a slum, in a little room that we made out of cardboard and plastic that we found. We have some pots and pans for cooking, a stone for grinding, and some bedding in our one room cardboard home. We each have one change of clothes. We have our dirty clothes to wear for trash picking and our clean clothes for when we get home. We've made friends in our slum group, and we all look out for each other when we can. Aaie, Arjun, Santosh, Ashok, and I all are rag pickers. We pair up with other kids in our slum when we go to different areas to trash pick. We stick together because some kids have been stolen while out trash picking. This scares us, and Aaie. She makes us promise to never go with anyone in a car or in a house, and to run away yelling for help. Aaie is always tired and feels bad for us because this is a hard life. I miss hearing my Aaie laugh. I still have trouble sleeping and the nightmare of my Baba dying keeps happening in my sleep.

My friend, Priyanka, and I work the same areas together. We keep an eye out for each other, and if we get some food at houses we share it. Some people in the houses know us and leave us leftover food they were going to throw out. We're happy to get the leftover food. Other houses don't trust us. The people yell at us and throw things. They think we tell robbers what we see so they can steal from them. Priyanka and I don't do that. Sometimes, police yell at us too. When that happens we move to another area because there are a lot of places to pick trash here.

Today started like any other day. We all had a small breakfast of chapati and chai. We changed into our rag picking clothes, grabbed our bags and left. We leave while it is still dark out and walk to the areas we can find to work. Priyanka and I work hard all morning looking through trash. We both know we can't go back until our bags are full. No one gave us food to eat so we put our bags by a building where we can see them, and start to beg for money. Today we're lucky, we get enough rupees to buy something to share from a street vendor. We eat very fast, then get back to work.

People living under a bridge just like Diya's family

The bag gets heavy as the day goes along. I keep it slung over my shoulder, so my shoulder starts to hurt. I've found some bottles today and that's very good because they will get me seven rupees (twelve cents). It's getting late, and Priyanka yells to me that her bag is almost full. I yell back that mine is too. Soon we walk back to sort what we have and get paid. I give Aaie the money when I get home. I'm so dirty, and my hair is a mess. This is filthy dirty work. Aaie tells me to go wash up and change my clothes. I also wash my rag picking clothes, then help Aaie make dinner. We all sleep inside our cardboard home huddled together. We barely fit in here. Some nights Arjun sleeps outside, but I never leave Aaie's side at night.

Age Eight

Another day of trash picking begins. Priyanka and I go to a trash pile and pick through the trash with the cows and pigs. It's a hot day but that's better than during monsoon time when it rains. We have trouble trash picking in the down pour. It's a normal day, but later a car drives by and then slows down. I think this is strange. I hope it's not a policeman stopping to yell at me for working in this area. The car backs up, and the man asks me if I'd like a ride because my bag looks heavy. I tell him no, just like Aaie has taught me. I walk away quickly from the car. The man gets out and starts to yell for me to stop, and says he wants to talk to me. I start to scream and run. Luckily, a woman in a house comes out to help. The man turns back and drives away in his car.

I find Priyanka and tell her what happened. We stay close together and watch for the car. When we're sure he's gone, we finish filling our bags. I can't stop shaking, and I'm afraid he's waiting to grab me somewhere. We know children that have disappeared and been stolen from our slum. Priyanka and I talk about this man, and how no one protects slum children, not even the police. I was lucky that woman helped me. We also talk about how some families in our slum have sold their daughters into prostitution for money to feed their families. We're glad our Aaie's haven't done that to us. I'm very scared and want to hurry home to Aaie to tell her all that happened.

We finish our day and go to the garbage collection center to sort and turn in what we gathered. I made thirty rupees (fifty cents). We hurry home and I tell Aaie what happened. She's glad I yelled and ran. She thinks I should be on alert in case the man comes back. We discuss all of this as Aaie is cooking dinner. I'm not hungry tonight because the stench from the trash has taken away my appetite. I go and wash, scrubbing my fingernails to remove the debris. I wash my hair and then brush it out. I hate how messy my hair is and how filthy dirty I am. I go back to our room and go right to sleep. I rarely have nightmares about Baba's death anymore.

There's a pastor from a Christian church who's been talking with Aaie. He tells her about Jesus, and how He can help us. Aaie talks about us going to this church to learn more. I think maybe this is just another god to worship that does nothing. We start to attend church on Sunday, and I like the music and the stories. Aaie accepts Jesus as her Savior and becomes a Christian. She is happier and laughs more now. The church helps us with clothes and things we need. The pastor discusses helping to get my brothers back into school. He knows of a home that has openings and would be glad to take my brothers. They would live there ten months of the year and have three meals a day, clothes, school fees, uniforms, and books. Also, they would go to a Christian church. Aaie is not sure about my brothers leaving though. If they were in school their lives would be better, but she tells the pastor we need their money as rag pickers to survive.

Slum homes of rag pickers. Large white bags filled with items found searching through trash in the city

He tells her maybe he could get her steady work as a pot scrubber. That would enable her to care for herself and me while the boys went to school. The boys are not sure about leaving and going to school, either. They want us to stay together. Aaie decides we should visit this home to see where the boys would live and go to school. The pastor takes us there. It's very nice. There are only boys in this home, of all ages. There are house parents who live there to take care of them. They have food, clothes, and school uniforms. Also, the children all play games, study the Bible, and get to go to church. The boys stay here until they pass their Standard Ten (10th grade) exams. If they're good, they can get help with Junior College, or a Technical School. Aaie makes the decision that if the pastor gets her steady work as a pot scrubber then the boys will go to the home.

The boys have mixed feelings about leaving though. Ashok never has been in school and only knows living on the streets. Then the pastor tells Aaie there's another home now accepting girls, and that I can live there through Standard Ten too. He says that even though we'll be in two different homes, she can visit us on Sundays. The homes are in different parts of town but they're both good Christian children's homes. I don't want to leave my Aaie, and I don't want my brother's to leave either. I want us all to be together.

Age Nine

I'm moving into New Beginnings Children's Home. My brothers are also moving into their new home. Aaie now works as a pot scrubber. It's scary to move here. The pastor, Aaie, and my brothers all come to move me into this home. There are also boys here and I ask why my brothers can't come here too. I'm told the home is full so they can't take any more boys. When Aaie and my brothers have to leave, I cry and hug them goodbye.

Aaie tells me she will come to visit me and I will see my brothers when we're all together for break.

I'm one of the first girls to be brought here and I have a sponsor in the U.S. who is paying for me to live here and go to school. There are around fifteen boys living here and four other girls. There are house parents that live here to help take care of me, and cooks that prepare the food. I'm told I'll have chores to do, but plenty of time to play. They have games for us to play here too. I'm introduced to everyone and shown to my room. I have a bedroll and a trunk to keep my things in. There is a shower and bathroom. We are all to brush our teeth. There is clean water to drink and plenty of food. I just hope I never have to pick trash again.

I've never gone to school, and I am used to being free on the streets all day. It's very hard to get used to all the rules here. I'm angry that Aaie left me here and it makes me cry. There are too many rules here, and I'm having trouble following them all.

I've lived here for four weeks now and it's getting better. The chores are very easy and I get to eat three times a day. The food is very good and there is plenty to eat. Aaie has come to visit me once. We had a good time playing and laughing together. She wanted to hear everything that I'm doing and learning. I still have trouble following the rules, but I think this is better for me than being a rag picker.

Age Fourteen

I have lived at New Beginnings Children's Home for five years now, and I'm in Standard Five. I am a good student and get some A's and B's in my classes. I've decided I would like to be a police officer when I am done with school. As a police officer, I'd work to protect and help the poor people, along with the children, living in the slums and on the streets. I'd arrest the guys who steal kids from the slums and stop them from hurting them and the poor people.

I have many favorite things now. My favorite color is red and I enjoy school. My favorite things to do at school are to study English, and, talk or dance with friends at recess. I study hard in English so if I ever meet my sponsor I can talk with them. Now I can even write letters to my sponsors in English. I have a bed now and I keep my bedding clean. I am always clean now. The chores I do here are not hard or dirty work. I teach the younger girls to do laundry and keep themselves clean too. I try to be patient and gentle with the younger kids and help them. All food is my favorite food. I help in the kitchen with the cooking and I've learned to cook many dishes. I find nothing about living here hard now. I am happy to share that I no longer have any nightmares.

Every May I go home to live with my Aaie and see my brothers. Arjun is nineteen now and he is in Standard Ten. He will be taking his exams and moving out of the children's home he's been living in. Santosh is twelve and he's in Standard Seven. Ashok is nine and in Standard Three. Aaie now has steady employment as a dishwasher in a restaurant. She lives in a small apartment outside of the slums. When I'm home with her I clean the rooms, do the laundry, and cook for her and my brothers. Aaie works hard all day, so I'm glad to have dinner ready for her when she comes home, so she can rest. We all attend church together on Sunday.

Most of all, I love Jesus now. He is my caregiver, Lord and Savior. Also, I'm getting ready to be baptized. I pray to Him to watch over Aaie and my brothers. I ask Him to give me the fruits of the Spirit: love, joy, peace, patience, kindness, goodness, faith, gentleness, and self-control. My favorite verse from the Bible is Hebrews 13:5: "God has said, 'Never will I leave you; never will I forsake you.'"

Diya singing in morning worship

Diya spending time with and talking to another girl and one of the house mothers at New Beginnings Children's Home

About meeting Diya

The first child we saw at New Beginnings Children's Home was Diya. She came barreling down the stairs with enough energy for ten children. She is 100 percent energy. She ran up and hugged us, then helped carry our things to our room. She was always ready to give a helping hand. Diya is a one of the cleanest children you will ever meet. She plays hard, then runs straight in to freshen up which includes washing and fixing her hair. She does not like to be dirty or to have messy hair. She shared with us that as a rag picker her hair was very messy, and that she always came home smelly and dirty. When we asked her to draw a picture about her life or of something she liked, she drew a self-portrait of her as a rag picker.

In India, statistics indicate that around 2 percent of any city's population consists of rag pickers, and of that 2 percent, children make up 10 to 30 percent of the rag pickers.[6] So, in a city the size of Mumbai with 19,291,439 people,[7] there are between 38,580 and 115,748 children living as rag pickers. According to India's law, it is illegal for children to be workers, however, almost every child we interviewed has been a paid worker. Unfortunately, in India, labor is unorganized and even though laws exist prohibiting child labor, there is virtually no enforcement. Diya worked to survive. It wasn't that her mother did not work too. The whole family worked as rag pickers to bring in around 100 rupees a day, or $1.65 a day. On a good week, they would make $11.55 for the entire week to care for a family of five.

We traveled through eight different cities in India and always saw children carrying their big white bags searching through

---

6 Lahiri, Ankita "Will someone pick up the rag pickers?"false *DNA Syndication* [Mumbai] Nov 14, 2011: http://goo.gl/ckxWCf

7 "Mumbai Population 2014" *World Population Review* March 15, 2014: http://worldpopulationreview.com/world-cities/mumbai-population/

garbage, just like Diya described, in towns large and small. Sometimes, we would leave very early before daybreak and see children with their empty bags getting started. Later, when we returned to our room for the night, we would see the children with full bags, ending their day. These children work long hard days just to earn enough for a small amount of food to survive.

Diya is constantly moving and working. From her years of trash picking, she has developed a strong work ethic. She also loves to dance, play games, and have clean clothes and bedding. We found her multiple times washing her clothes and bedding. She even wanted me to notice how clean and fresh her bed is after she washed her wool blanket. Food is very important to Diya. Every conversation we had with her somehow ended up around food. She does not like to be hungry and enjoys eating. She did not care for the food we bought, peanut butter and crackers, she said it did not have enough flavor.

Her mother and brothers are very important to her too. She lights up when her mother comes to visit. There was a year-end school performance at her school in which she danced while we were there. Her mother came to see her dance which made Diya's day that she would take time off of work to come see her.

Diya and her friends playing a parachute game

Diya's self-portrait of her time as a rag picker. She wanted us to see how messy her hair was after filling the large trash picker bag

Diya dressed to perform in the year-end school dance

Jesus is very important to Diya. In this unreached country, it is refreshing to be in a place where Jesus is not just proclaimed, but where He is loved. Diya sincerely loves Jesus. She believes with her whole heart He is always with her. She quoted from Hebrews by memory. In church Diya is always paying attention. She prays with abandon and sings with great joy. Diya is preparing for her baptism. Her mother is a Christian and this gives us great hope that Diya will have a Christian future.

Diya is also a very giving girl. She wore special earrings for her dance that her mother had given her. She gave me those earrings as a gift to always remember her. I didn't want to take them, but the house parents told me that the children are taught to give as well as receive, and that I should accept Diya's gift. I will always remember Diya and cherish her gift.

When asked what she would like us to share with the children in America, Diya replied, "Please give my best wishes to all the children of America!"

Diya playing with one of the goats at the children's home

Diya helping clean up after some of the construction work on the children's home

Diya resting out in the field behind the children's home

Aman

Newborn

My parents tell me when I was born everyone was very happy because a son was born. My parents had a girl child first and were hoping I'd be a boy child. There is always great happiness when a boy child is born in our village, but not as much happiness at a girl child's birth. I'm told that I was named Nagesh, which means "snake," because I had a long thin body and a big head. Aaie said Nana and Nani were concerned about the way I looked. Aaie was sure I would grow up and be fine.

I was born on a farm in a small village where my family lives with Nani and Nana. Baba and Aaie are farmers and work all day long with Nani and Nana in the fields. My sister, Sani, is six years old and helps take care of me. We are all very close in our farm village.

Age Four

I don't like loud noise. Yelling and banging noises make me hide. I like to play quietly alone or with my sister. My favorite things to do are to sit and rock, and be with my sister. Sometimes I hit and throw things at my family, or other people. Nani says I act crazy. I hear her tell my Aaie that she will take me and deal with me. Aaie tells her no, that I will learn to behave better. I feel bad when I throw things or hit. I just can't seem to stop. My sister goes to school now. I hope that I can behave when I go to school and not be crazy. People in our village don't like me to be around. I can tell that they don't want me around. They say I look wrong and act crazy. Some people say I'm possessed by demons. My parents are concerned with my acting crazy. Aaie asks me why I do this and why I don't behave better. Baba just looks at me and walks away. I don't know why I do these things. I don't think I can help it.

Age Seven

Now I'm a big brother. Aaie and Baba have had another son, Chottu. I think I will like being an older brother. I like helping Aaie with work in our home and I will help take care of Chottu too. Maybe I can give him my old clothes and teach him to play cricket. I like to play cricket. I watch the boys play cricket, and sometimes I play too. I have trouble playing with the boys in my village. They make fun of me, and when they call me names, I run and hide or sit and rock. Nani says I act crazy. I start school this year and am excited to go with my sister. Aaie said not to rock, throw things, or act crazy at school. I hear "crazy" a lot – I must be.

I've been at school for a week now. It's very hard. I try to act ok, but the other kids make fun of me and ask me why I act strange. They say I am a demon. The more they call me names the angrier I get, and I can't help myself. I run into a corner, and sit rocking and pounding. The teacher tells me to stop it and to get back in my seat. I can't sit in my seat. I wish they could understand. The teacher hits me and makes me sit at my desk. The other two boys I share a desk with call me names. I wish they would leave me alone.

I went to school for a couple of weeks. The school told Aaie and Baba that I couldn't go to school there. I did not like the kids making fun of me and calling me names. I also did not like my teacher hitting me. I'm glad that I don't have to go to school, and be called names and hit by the teacher.

Baba has also stopped taking me to market. I have a hard time in the large crowd. I start to get scared and then I act crazy. Baba says it's best if I just stay at home with Aaie and Nani.

Nani and Aaie are talking. I hear Nani telling Aaie it would be better if I was dead, and she should just poison me. She says, "What kind of life will he have? No one will ever marry him." Aaie tells her no, that I am her son and she knows with time I will be better.

Age Eight

Baba and Aaie say we must leave our village. They pack our things and tell us we're moving to the city. They think I don't know why we are leaving, but I do. Nani wants to kill me and the villagers agree with her. Aaie told Baba that we have to leave to protect me. Baba does not want to leave his parents, or the village. They talk for many days and finally decide that we should go.

We are moving far from our village to a large city. We hope that Baba and Aaie can find work in the city. Aaie says there will be no farms in the city, but there will be factories where she and Baba hope to find work.

I'm not sure if I'll like the city. Aaie tells me it's bigger than the market. We're going to take everything we own with us and get on a train. Nani is upset that we're leaving, and there have been many arguments about the move.

I hope I'll be better in the city. Maybe I can try another school, if there's one that will be nice to me and kids that won't call me names. Maybe I can even find kids that will let me play cricket with them. Aaie, Baba, Sani, Chottu, and I leave to go to the train station. I'm glad to be leaving.

Once we get to the city, things become hard. It is very crowded and noisy. I start feeling worse. We live in the slums because Aaie and Baba can't find work. We all become rag pickers. I don't like looking through the garbage for metal, plastic, paper, and rags. Aaie goes with me and we work together. That does help me some.

The work is very dirty and we work seven days a week picking trash. We barely make enough money to feed our family. All of us, even Chottu, work at going through the trash. I get in a lot of fights in the slums. Aaie is concerned because every day she says I get wilder. She tries to help me calm down.

Age Ten

I don't like the city. I don't like going into the crowds in the large markets. I like the side areas around our slum. I have some kids I play cricket with when we're done filling our bags of trash for the day. I don't go to school because none of the kids in the slum go to school. I get in fights almost every day. My Aaie says I am wild and is worried about me.

Every day we work to have just enough food to feed ourselves. There is a pastor that comes to our slum to talk with people. He likes to pray for us and he tells us about a God named Jesus. He has invited our family to attend church. Aaie is very excited to go see this church. Baba, Aaie, Sani, Chottu, and I all go to the church that's in a small room at a school in our city. There's music and singing. Pastor speaks and I find I can pay real good attention.

The other kids and I sit in the front of the room. All I notice is Pastor and what he is teaching. Some of the boys have trouble sitting and mess around, but I am pleased that I don't. I can tell Pastor is pleased with me.

Pastor visits with my family often. He teaches us about Jesus and how He died for our sins. Aaie and Baba discuss me with Pastor and how I behave crazy at times. I wish they wouldn't tell him that. They share with him why we left our village. Pastor says he will pray for me and help teach me. I like Pastor very much. He is kind to me. He teaches me manners and not to fight. He also has taught me how to write my name, Nagesh.

As we all learn about Jesus we each decide to become Christians. One by one, we are all baptized. When Pastor baptized me, we changed my name from Nagesh to Aman. Aman means "peace." Pastor does not think it is good for me to be named for Nageshwaran, the Hindu god-snake. I like Aman very much and hope it helps me to be even more peaceful.

Age Twelve

Pastor says he can help us get jobs at a brick-making factory. We no longer work as rag pickers looking through the trash. At the brick factory, we're given a room for our family to live in. I'm very glad for our room. In the slum, we had a cardboard and plastic home. It would get cold and wet. Now, we'll be dry living in this room at the brick factory. In order to pay the owner for the room we have to make bricks. We have an account with the owner, who tracks our rent and any money we get to buy clothes or food. We have to make enough bricks to pay the owner back. Then, whatever money we make for extra bricks is ours to spend. We get 600 rupees for each 1,000 bricks we make. On a good day, we can make between 700-800 bricks. This is very good for our family. The first couple thousand bricks pay back the brick factory owner.

It is expected by the factory owner that the entire family work to pay for our room. I work from 8:00 o'clock in the morning until 8:00 o'clock at night. Aaie says I am strong to work twelve hours a day. I like making bricks. My favorite part is mixing the mud and sand. I like to run my hands through the mud and sand, and mix it very well. It relaxes me and makes me feel good, not angry. Aaie and Baba take turns making the bricks with Chottu and me. We fill the mold and then they turn the mold out onto the ground for the bricks to dry. We make neat rows of bricks to dry. They do this for a few hours, and then Chottu and I dump the bricks while they fill the mold. We have a number three in our mold so the owner knows which bricks our family has made. It's hard work, but it makes me peaceful.

Baba spends money on gambling and drinking. He and Aaie fight about his drinking. He says that's how he handles the way we live. Baba misses his family and farm life. Aaie tells him we are his family and that I am doing better all the time. She says he is using me as an excuse for his bad habits.

Pastor still teaches me. We work on writing my name. He is using a Bible to teach me to read. He tells me it's important for me to help Aaie with cooking and fetching water. Most importantly, he tells me things about Jesus. He is pleased that I am working hard and learning to behave better. He tells me that Jesus is helping me to be good and peaceful – just like Jesus is all good and peaceful.

Age Fourteen

I still work at making bricks with my family. We work in a different factory now but the work is the same. My week is busy with work Monday through Saturday. I've made friends at the factory, and after church on Sunday, Chottu and I play cricket with them. I like to be a hitter. I'm one of the best hitters. Aaie says this is because I'm very strong. Chottu likes to follow me around. I teach him how to play cricket and fetch water. I look out for Chottu and am a good older brother.

Sani is grown up and married now. She has a little girl. They work in the brick factory with us too. I am glad that Sani is still with us. She loves me and helps me to calm down. Sani has always loved me and helped Aaie care for me. Sani teaches me to cook different foods. My favorite thing to cook, and eat, is chapati and chicken. Aaie likes me helping her with the cooking.

Baba left us for six months a while back. It was a very hard time for our family. With Baba gone, we could not make as many bricks. We had to work much harder. Pastor found Baba and talked with him. He was able to help Aaie and Baba so that Baba could come back home. I'm glad, we need Baba. Pastor also talked with Baba about gambling and drinking alcohol. Pastor has taught me not to do these things too, even though other people in the brickyard do. It is bad to drink alcohol and makes you not peaceful. Gambling takes the money we work hard to make and is like throwing it away. I listen to Pastor and stay away from these things.

I have decided that when I grow up I will be a pastor. I love Jesus. In church, I'm very peaceful and able to be well-mannered. I sing the songs, pray, and listen to all that the pastors teach us. My favorite thing is to pray. It makes me peaceful. Pastor is pleased that I don't mess around in church like the other boys. I sit very still, participate, and listen. Even though I do not go to school, I'm sure I will be a pastor when I grow up. Pastor tells me that I won't have a degree like the other pastors, but the Heavenly Father is more powerful than all those degrees and that He will keep His blessings on me. I think it is important for me to be a pastor in order to help other people, like Pastor has helped me.

Aman working at making bricks in the brickyard where his family lives and works

The bricks are neatly laid out in rows to dry

About meeting Aman

The first child we interviewed in India was Aman. We were invited to attend church our first full day in India. At the church service, we were surprised when I was asked to give a message. As I spoke, I noticed a muscular young man in the kid section who was paying very close attention. While some of the other teens whispered or messed around, this young man was completely engaged in the service. I felt a prompting to meet this child and talk with him.

When asked if we could possibly stay after church to meet with him, we were told he had a very interesting story. We learned that no one exactly knows what makes Aman different. As grandparents of a child with Asperger's Syndrome, we were quite sure after spending time with Aman, that he has some form of Autism. That would explain some of what his mother calls "crazy behavior." Our hearts were torn apart for this child as his mother shared with us the repeated attempts on his life by his paternal grandmother. This grandmother was set on killing him. She even went as far as to give his mother poison to put in his ear, telling her it would kill him in his sleep.

We are so thankful that his mother went the distance to save her son's life. She is a very strong mother and believes God has a purpose for her son's life. She believed this even before she was a Christian. We were amazed at the coping techniques Aman developed all on his own. He and his mother shared how much making bricks helped him focus and gave him peace. As he described how he felt mixing the mud and sand, and letting it run between his fingers, I pictured our grandson running his hands through the rice in the rice table at his school. I think it's horrible that this child has to work twelve hours a day making bricks. Although, as he described how mixing the brick mud and laying rows of bricks gives him peace, I found myself thanking God for giving him this special work.

Aman's story represents a serious children's issue in India. In some areas, children born with a mental or physical disability are either killed or made to beg in the streets to help support their families. Their disability is considered as punishment for wrongdoing in a past life. It's believed they must pay for that wrongdoing. Children with mental disorders are simply murdered, especially in the rural farm communities. We asked if there are any programs or services for children with mental disorders, and were told they are rare in India. It brings dishonor upon the family to have a child with a physical or mental disorder. Aman's family deals with this separation every day of their lives, having been driven from their family and farming village.

Aman waiting for his turn to have communion

There are no school or government school programs for children in India with special needs. The options for a future are slim. Since all marriages are arranged in India, a child with a mental or physical disability will not be chosen as a suitable mate, because this individual's disability is believed to be punishment from a past wrongdoing. Aman's mother and father do not believe he will ever be married or have a family. They say he'll be with them for his entire life. Then when they are gone, they hope his sister will care for him.

We discussed school with Aman at length. Wondering if we found a school somewhere that could help him, we asked if he would go. Aman said he would go back to school if the children there wouldn't call him names, and if the teachers wouldn't hit him. He enjoys the pastor teaching him to write his name and read the Bible. He's concerned that he won't be able to be a pastor because if he can't go to school, he can't go to Bible College.

It is hard manual labor that Aman and his family do every single day. The hot sun beats down on them as they work long repetitive hours mixing, filling, molding, and lining up bricks to dry in the sun. I asked Aman if they stopped to eat and drink during the day, and he shared that yes they do, one time. Aman never once complained about his work. He is glad to have this job because it helps calm him. He says it makes him very peaceful to work there. The family shared they feel blessed to have this work and not be rag pickers any longer.

We were able to get permission to go to the brickyard and visit Aman's home, and see the bricks he makes. Aman and his family live in a small one room brick compound in the brick factory yard, where they hang their laundry out to dry and cook over a fire outside the opening to their room. During the monsoon season, brick making stops, and they have to live in debt to the brick factory owner for being allowed to stay on the premises. This requires them to work off the debt when the season ends and brick making resumes. It's an endless cycle, from which this family may never escape.

We asked Aman if he would color us a picture of something he likes or something important to him, so we could take it with us to share. He had never colored, or even drawn a picture before, so I took out the crayons and notebook to show him what I was asking. He laughed, and kept shaking his head at me. After some discussion with the translator, Aman agreed to try. We both sat down in the middle of the brickyard, then Aman drew a plant, his home, a cell phone, and a cross. We had to smile that even here, in the brickyard, the young boys want a cell phone. Every boy we spoke to in India was interested in having one.

Aman's niece plays making bricks while the family works

Room where Aman's family lives at the brickyard

Aman was so excited about his picture and took it to show to his family. We decided to leave the crayons and the rest of that notepad with Aman. When we asked him if he had a message to share with the children in America, he pointed to his picture. As we started to leave, Aman took my hand and held onto me very tightly. He was so proud that someone was taking an interest in his life and told him that he was important. We shared with Aman how very important he is – so important that Jesus brought us all the way to India to learn about his life and story. He had never been told before that he was important by anyone other than his mother and Pastor. We prayed over him, and as we left, Aman gave me a big hug goodbye. This surprised his parents because Aman usually avoids physical contact.

Unfortunately, this was the last time we saw Aman in India. We have heard from the pastor that he looks for us every Sunday and asks when we're coming back. We hope to return someday. We pray for God's blessing on this child and that he will continue to have peace in his life.

Aman smiling during his first meeting with us

Aman's picture of his important things – A brick, cross, tree, cell phone, and flower

Aman posing with his finished picture in the brickyard

Aman with his father, mother, and younger brother

Kala

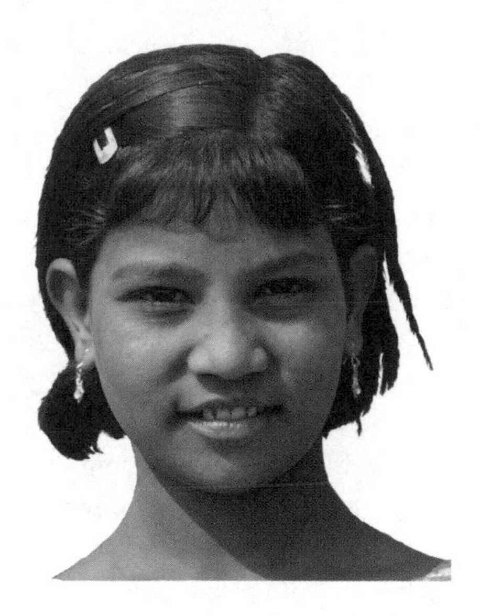

Age Eight

I am Kala. I live with Aaie and Baba along with my four older brothers, two older sisters, and one younger sister. We spend six months of the year harvesting sugarcane, then, the rest of the year we beg and are rag pickers. I prefer sugarcane harvesting to rag picking. We all work together every day with our Uncle, Aunty, and cousins. Our family has always been sugarcane harvesters. As Dalits, or Untouchables, we are glad to have this work. None of the children in our family go to school. We all work with our families to survive.

It's the start of the sugarcane season. We packed up our belongings and put them into our ox cart. A truck comes to pick us up and we ride in the back with our oxen and cart of belongings. Aaie tells me we're lucky to have the oxen because they help us with the heavy work. I think this is why the oxen are always fed first, even when we do not have food to eat. The truck travels a long distance away from the city and our slum home. I'm glad to be going out to the fields away from the noise and crowded city. We'll work long, hard days, but for a while at least we'll have money for food. The sharecropper manager we work for pays Baba for the six months in advance. At first, we have plenty of money for food, but it always runs out before we finish the season. Baba and my brothers drink and gamble, losing money as we go from farm to farm. So, in a few months, we'll not only have to work in the fields, but go out to beg for money or food too.

We arrive at the first field where we'll start working. We will work in many different fields during the season. When we finish at one farm, a truck comes to move us to the next, until the sugarcane season is over. Our home is moveable. We tear it down and bundle it up as we move from farm to farm, harvesting crops. At each field, we're given a spot to live and that's where we rebuild our home. We unpack and rebuild our hut. Our home is made of bamboo poles, plastic, and dried sugarcane leaves. The workers in our group build our huts in a row. At the end of the season, we go back to live in our slum.

There's a water pump at this farm and we're told we are allowed to use it. Some of the farmers make us use certain water pumps because we're Untouchables, from the Dalit caste. They don't want us using the same water as their families. I get water for the oxen and for Aaie to cook. Dinner tonight will be good. We have plenty of money for food at the start of the sugarcane season, so we have rice, dahl, and chapati tonight. Everyone is in good spirits at the camp. Tomorrow we will start early in the morning.

My day starts very early, while it is still dark. I go to the well that we're allowed to use to get water. I wash up with the cold water. Aaie starts to make us chai and chapati. To make the chapati she must grind the grains using a stone in front of our tent. She starts a fire with dried dung from our animals and some wood. She tells me to get the others up because we have a full workday. It is 4:00 a.m. when we start getting ready to work. We all drink our chai and then we take our cutting knives to harvest the sugarcane. I have my own knife that I've used since I could pick it up and glean in the fields. I think I was four years old when I started working in the fields. I wear my brother's old clothes. I do not have a saree, or other girl clothes, and I have no shoes. I have never had any shoes. My feet get cut by the sugarcane leaves and Aaie says that they will get tough. If I get a bad enough cut, Aaie will tie scrap cloth around my foot to help. To protect my arms and legs from the sugarcane leaves, I wear long sleeves and pants. It's very hot sometimes, but it's better than the sharp leaves cutting me.

My little sister, Rakhi, is five years old. She will glean in the fields with me today, and we will work together. After the others cut the long stalks and remove them, we crawl along the ground and cut from the bottom whatever is left of the sugarcane stalk. This is important work because we are allowed to keep and sell what we glean. This helps our family earn extra money for food.

We get a one-hour break for water and some food. This early in the season we have enough money that there is dahl to go with our rice for lunch. Aaie asks us to cut some sugarcane leaves and give them to the oxen to eat. I am careful not to get cut by the sharp leaves from the stalks. The sharp leaves do not seem to bother the oxen. They eat them right up. We have painted our oxen's horns to celebrate Mattu Pongal, which is our celebration of the oxen, and the start of the harvest. We appreciate all the hard work the oxen do during the harvest, so we celebrate on January 15th, at the start of the season. Aaie tells me we're lucky to have our oxen to haul our sugarcane because it helps us clear the fields faster. We take good care of our two oxen. After lunch, we ride in the ox cart back to the field where we're working. Rakhi and I work side by side until evening. While Aaie, Rakhi, and I get dinner ready, everyone else gets the cart loaded with the sugarcane we harvested today. The sugarcane that Rakhi and I harvested will be saved, and we'll try to sell it ourselves at market or along the road to get some extra money.

My brothers will wait at the road until the truck comes for our sugarcane. They'll load it into the truck and then come back to camp for dinner. Sometimes they wait until well into the night for the truck to come. Today the truck came at 9:00 p.m. The oxen are unyoked from the cart and fed sugarcane leaves for their dinner. Dinner tonight is rice, dahl, and chapati. We had three meals today. It is a good day. We have plenty to eat because it's the start of the sugarcane harvesting season, but the rest of the year we'll eat only one meal a day, or have to beg for food.

Rakhi and I, as the youngest, will go out begging for food or money. People don't like to give us food or money because we are Dalits. Sometimes we get hit or kicked when we're begging. I don't like to beg but we have to, or we don't eat. Aaie has told us that we need to be careful and look out for each other. So, when we're out begging, I look out for Rakhi.

It's been a long season and we're at the last farm. Tomorrow we'll go back to our slum in the city. Sometimes our Baba and brothers will get work since we have two oxen and a cart hauling things. We mainly survive by being rag pickers, begging, or cleaning latrines. Our slum is right next to a school. Sometimes, I watch all the children go to school in their uniforms. I wonder what it would be like to not have to search through the trash, and get to go to the school instead. I see their mothers come at lunchtime with their buckets of food, and bags of water or milk for their lunch. I think it would be nice to get to go to school. I've heard adults say there are programs that allow Dalit children to go to school with government funding. But, I have to help work with my family so we can survive. None of the children in my family get this help to go to school.

We are back at our slum home. Baba tells us we need to get to work rag picking. He is drinking more and has been complaining about pain in his ear and chest. Baba never plays with us. He rarely talks with us, other than to tell us to get to work. Rakhi and I leave to go picking through the trash to look for things like plastic, metal, glass, or rags that we can sell for money. The city is noisy with the horns always blowing from the cars and motorbikes. There are people everywhere and I miss the open fields of sugarcane. We beg for food as we go and today is good, because we get some old chapati from one of the houses. Rakhi and I fill our bags and take them to sort and sell at the garbage collection center. We make twenty rupees today. As we head home, I think of how Baba will use this to buy his alcohol. We get there and find Aaie upset. While we were gone, Baba died.

Age Nine

We are more dependent on my brothers now that Baba has died. Aaie met a pastor from the school next to our slum and she is now a Christian. The pastor helped us and brought some clothes so we could go to the church at the school next to our slum. He helped me get a saree to wear. The pastor talks to Aaie about Rakhi and I coming to live at a Christian home where we will be cared for and given an education. I don't want to go, but Aaie thinks it is a good idea. She thinks that my four brothers and older sister will be enough workers for the sugarcane season.

She thinks it will be good for us to get an education, clothes, food, and attend church. We visit New Beginnings Children's Home. The children all seem happy, but I don't want to stay. Aaie tells me this is better and she will visit when she can. Rakhi and I are left at the home.

It is hard here at the home. We have many rules we have to follow. Rakhi and I are not used to all these rules. We have to shower, wash our clothes, brush our teeth, attend morning exercises, attend morning devotions, eat breakfast, then go to school where the rules start all over again. School is very hard and I don't like it either. At the home the children have chores, but these are not too hard for Rakhi and me. We are used to working hard. We don't know the games the children play. We have never had toys or games to play. We learn to play carrom, a board game, and it quickly becomes my favorite thing to do at New Beginnings Children's Home.

I now have new clothes and shoes. I have play clothes to wear at the home and a uniform to wear for school. At school we have to wear a white shirt and a blue skirt with shoes. On Wednesday, we can wear whatever we want. I like Wednesday because I can wear any color I like even though blue is my favorite color. I have a bed in one of the girls' rooms where I sleep. I've never had a bed before where I'm up off the floor with a mattress and bed covers. Rakhi is in another room and she has a bed too. I used to sleep on the floor of our hut or outside on the ground. I start to like having a bed too.

I miss my brothers, sister, and Aaie very much, but it is nice to have three meals a day and games to play. The work is not hard here and it does not take much time to do our chores. I wonder how the sugarcane harvest is going and how my family is doing without Rakhi and me to glean the fields. School is getting easier and the children here help me with my studies in Standard One.

Gypsy home at a sugarcane camp like Kala and Rakhi's camp home

Small child ready to go work in the fields with a knife almost as big as she is tall

Age Eleven

Rakhi and I have lived at New Beginnings Children's Home for three years now. Aaie comes and visits us every three to four months. It is fun when she comes and sometimes we go to the small shop in town. We tell her about life here at the home, school, and what scriptures we are studying. The last time she visited, I told her all about what we were learning in my favorite subject, Science. We were learning about bones and the anatomy of the body. I shared with her that I'm thinking I would like to be a police officer when I grow up. She asked me why I would like to be a police officer. I tell her so that I can keep people safe and have a good job with a uniform. She is happy for us to be here and have a chance at a better life. She tells us our older sister is married to another sugarcane harvester. She is worried about my older brothers who are drinking and gambling. Aaie asks us to pray for them.

Kala with her best friend

Kala making sure she is seen in the photo too

Both Rakhi and I are in Standard Three, but with different teachers. I enjoy school and like to study. I have friends in school and like going Monday through Saturday. We get lunch every day at school and when we return to the home we have a snack. I am very glad to have a sponsor and live here. I no longer wish to leave the home and be back in the sugarcane fields. It's much better for us here. I love Sundays. Every Sunday we attend church. I've learned many lessons hearing the stories from the Bible. Jesus is my Savior and I am a Christian. No longer are we Dalits because there are no castes as a Christian.

About meeting Kala

There was a precious little girl that somehow got into almost every picture we took while at the children's home. She would just jump in every time the camera was out. That little girl was Kala. She is quick to smile and likes to be included in everything that is going on at the home. She plays hard, worships strong, and studies everything that is going on around her.

Rakhi at morning devotions

Kala talked with us quite a bit about what it is like to be from the Dalit, or Untouchable caste. In India, the caste system dictates all aspects of a person's life, from their education and job, to who they can marry. The caste system in India is broken down into main groups as follows:

Brahmin (Priests): Consists of those engaged in scriptural education and teaching; essential for the continuation of knowledge

Kshatriya (Warriors): Take on all forms of public service, including administration, maintenance of law and order, and defense Kshatriya

Viasya (Merchants, Landowners): Engage in commercial activity as businessmen or farmers

Shudra/Sudra (Commoners, Peasants, Servants): Work as semi-skilled and unskilled laborers

Dalit (Outcast, Untouchable): Survive as rag pickers, latrine cleaners, and farm workers

The caste system in India has existed for over 3,000 years. It is supposedly illegal, with laws to help those from lower castes get education and better jobs, but everyone we spoke with indicated the caste system still dictates a person's place in society. Those who try to take advantage of the programs to get themselves out of poverty face extreme discrimination from teachers, students, and co-workers. Even with the programs in place, it is hard for the poor to take advantage of them due to lack of funding for the school uniforms and supplies. These families need every able-bodied child working to help the family survive.

Kala making sure she gets in the photo while cleaning grain

As we traveled throughout India, in every city, we heard stories of girls being punished for falling in love with someone outside of their caste. In one newspaper article, a girl was hung by her brothers for eloping with a Dalit boy.[8] There were stories of Dalit girls being raped and Dalit boys being beaten. One of our

8 Dalit "Brothers hang to death 17-year-old girl for eloping with Dalit youth" *The Times of India* Sep 14, 2013: http://timesofindia.indiatimes.com/city/madurai/Brothers-hang-to-death-17-year-old-girl-for-eloping-with-dalit-youth/articleshow/22567045.cms

guides shared with us that his caste was the Kshatriya. He fell in love in University with a girl from the Brahmin caste. His parents refused to arrange a marriage between him and this young woman. Instead, they insisted he marry a girl from his own caste that he had never met. He was not happy but said he had to honor his parents. He shared that he is living in a different city and has left his wife with his father and mother. He will eventually have to move home, but for now he will live here where he works.

Being born into a low caste, which allows nothing else to determine what can be done with your life, is the life Kala was born into. She was in the worst possible place as an Untouchable. Her life would have been harvesting sugarcane and rag picking for as long as she lived, married to another Dalit sugarcane picker, if a pastor had not reached out into the gypsy camp and shared Jesus with her mother. Kala wanted us to understand how hard life was for her before she came to New Beginnings Children's Home. When I told her that I had never seen sugarcane growing, she drew me a picture of sugarcane and the knife she used to glean the fields. She showed me her arms, legs, and feet that had scars from where the sugarcane leaves had cut her.

We had an opportunity to visit both the sugarcane camp where Kala would have been working and the slum next to the school where she lived in the off-season. At the sugarcane camp, each family had a small tent-like hut they lived in which moved with them from farm to farm. Everything these families owned was right there with them and portable. The children in the sugarcane camp worked alongside their families in the fields all day long. Even the little children walked around carrying the harvesting knives that were just as long as they were tall. This is all these children know of life and maybe all they will know. When we were at the slum, we saw it was right next door to a beautiful school. I wonder how the children in the slum must feel to be right next door hearing the children play and learn. To watch them go in everyday with their uniforms and backpacks while they go off begging and rag picking through the trash. It was hard for me to picture Kala and Rakhi here in these places. It was hard to see the children still living in these places.

Food is very important to Kala. She talked about every meal and snack she gets every day between the home and school. She was always one of the first in the kitchen at meal time. When we asked what she would like to share with the children in America, she wanted me to share that she loves Chicken Biryani. This is a traditional Indian dish the children have for Christmas dinner at the home. She loves to play kho kho, which is a game similar to tag. In church, I observed her paying very close attention and singing loudly. Kala touched my heart when she shared that she is no longer untouchable, and that there is no caste in Christianity. She shared that in Christianity all are equal in God's eyes.

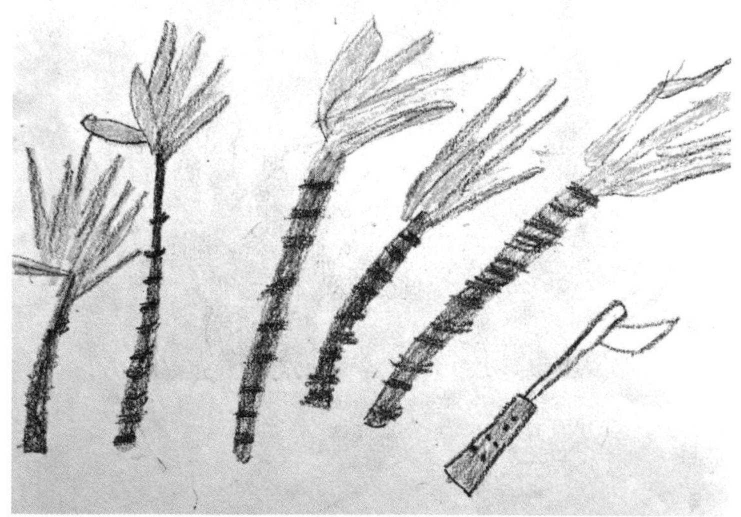

Kala drew a picture of sugarcane and the knife she used to glean the fields

Kala and Rakhi

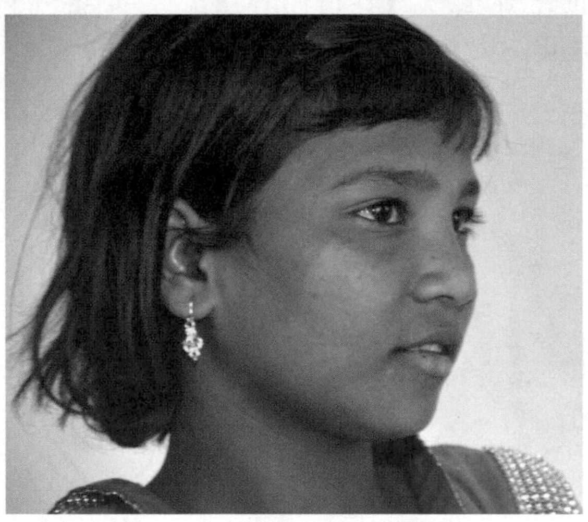

Kala during our interview at New Beginnings Children's Home

Kala playing "Hey Girl" with her friends

Leena

Newborn

I was the firstborn to my family. Since I've seen the births of my three sisters, I can tell you that there was no joy at my birth. I was viewed immediately by Baba as a burden. A dowry would have to be paid for me to be married someday. Every time a new daughter has come into our family Baba has been very angry with Aaie for not producing a son. Girl children are very expensive to an Indian family. In our country, there is great rejoicing at the birth of a son but not so much at a daughter, especially in our home. I was named Leena, which means "tender" in Hindi.

Baba and Aaie work as construction workers. I am left behind with Nani when Aaie goes to work with Baba when I am one year old. Aaie has to work to help earn my dowry. I stay with Nani during the day, and go with her to her work as a pots and pans washer. Nani is very kind to me. She is Baba's Aaie and she is pleased to have granddaughters, despite Baba's feelings.

Age Two

Aaie was with child again when I was twenty months old. She prayed to the Hindu gods to make this baby a son to make Baba pleased with her. The Hindu gods must not have heard her. She gave birth to another daughter, Chandani, which means "moon" in Hindi. I thought Chandani was very beautiful with her light brown hair and dark brown eyes. Her hair was much lighter than mine. I help with Chandani and love to be with my baby sister.

Baba was again not pleased with Aaie and he yelled at her for bringing him another daughter. There was no happiness at Chandani's birth. Aaie cried and Baba was upset. Nana and Nani were quiet. Nani takes care of us when Aaie goes back to construction work. Nani and Aaie take good care of us girls.

Age Five

Aaie is pregnant again and the baby is due soon. I pray with Aaie to the Hindu gods every Wednesday for the birth of a healthy baby boy. Baba says Aaie has bad karma and that is why she is bringing only daughters into our family. Aaie tells Nani that she is fearful that Baba will leave her because of her bad karma. Nani tells her things will be fine. Aaie looks worried as she carries this baby.

I spend my time helping and playing with Chandani. We love to play with pots and pans while Nani washes. I also like to play kho kho and have fun with other kids. Chandra follows me everywhere and I don't mind. I also like to brush Chandani's hair. Chandani loves the color red. She has a beautiful red saree that she likes to wear. We have fun together.

Another daughter has been born. This sister is named

Somatra, which means "moon rays" in Hindi. Aaie is very quiet and Baba is very upset. The light is gone from Aaie's eyes. She doesn't even seem to see us. Baba says Aaie has bad karma and he leaves. Aaie cries and stares at nothing. Nani tries to help and encourages her to take care of Somatra. Nani helps take care of us. I keep Chandani busy and help her bathe, dress, eat, and play.

Baba finally comes home, but things seem different. Aaie tells me I have to go to work at the construction site with Baba so she can care for Somatra. I don't wish to go to work with Baba at the construction site. At the construction site I do whatever they tell me. I carry things to different places, help pick up things and clean up as I'm told. I told Aaie I did not like going to the construction work and she beat me. After a few beatings, I learned to stay quiet about not liking work and to just go to work. I missed spending my day playing with Chandani.

Aaie has really changed. She is quick to beat us and her eyes are different. The light is gone from them. Baba and her fight about many things. Ours is not a home with joy.

Age Seven

Another daughter, Nakusa, has been born. Nakusa means "unwanted" in Hindi. Baba has left us and told us he will not be back. Aaie is very, very upset. She does not take care of Nakusa, Somatra, or Chandani. I am now age seven, Chandani is five, Somatra is two, and Nakusa is one month old. This time Baba is not coming back. When Nakusa was born he told Aaie they are divorced, and he wishes a new wife with better karma. Baba left and we are now alone. Aaie goes out and leaves me to take care of my sisters. She does not look right to me and Baba called her crazy when he left. I think maybe she has gone crazy.

Things are very hard for us. I try to play with Chandani and Somatra when I am not working at the construction site. Aaie leaves us alone a lot. I help feed my sisters and dress them. I miss Baba too. Sometimes he would spend time teaching me about the game of cricket. I don't understand why he did not like his daughters. I don't understand why he left us all alone with Aaie being like this and even Nani doesn't come around when Aaie is home to check on us. We go to bed and Aaie goes out. She is always back when I wake up in the morning. I get up and help with my sisters before I go to the construction site to work.

Today was a long day of work. We all go to sleep and I am looking forward to rest tonight. I wake up suddenly because Chandani is thrashing in her sleep. As I sit up I slowly back up against the wall trying to understand what I am seeing. I feel fear rise up in me. Aaie is choking Chandani around her neck. Suddenly Chandani stops moving. Aaie continues to hold her hands around her neck for a while. I am scared and can't move. My heart is pounding in my chest and I am shaking all over. I can't tell as I look if Somatra and Nakusa are asleep or dead. I am sure Aaie has killed Chandani. I am terrified.

Aaie stands up and turns towards me. Her eyes are strange and I don't know what to do as she keeps coming towards me. I am against the wall and can't move. Suddenly I yell, "Aaieee can I get you water, Aaieee please let me get you a drink of water!" Aaie stops moving towards me and just stares at me. Her eyes seem to change and then she turns away from me. I stay against the wall shaking but not moving. My heart still pounding so hard I am sure Aaie can hear it. She wraps Nakusa in a saree. She wraps Somatra in a saree. She wraps Chandani in her red saree. The same saree I love to dress Chandani in because it is her favorite. Then she carries each of them away from our room. I don't know what she is doing with them but I know they are all dead.

Leena during one of our interviews with her

Leena's picture of her home at New Beginnings Children's Home

Aaie comes back and says nothing to me. I am still against the wall scared, shaking, and not sure what to do. Aaie lays down and goes to sleep. I stay there until morning, scared and crying. In the morning Aaie gets up and starts screaming, "My daughters, my daughters – someone has stolen my daughters!" All over our area everyone is concerned and looking for Chandani, Somatra, and Nakusa. I say nothing and people think I am scared of being stolen too. Nani comes and asks me what happened. I tell her I don't know.

I am scared and Aaie is acting different. She is drinking alcohol and people are saying she is a prostitute. Nani is very concerned for me because of my Aaie being a prostitute. Nani talks with Aaie and she agrees to let me go stay with Nani. Once I'm at Nani's building, I feel safer. That night I tell Nani everything I saw. I was hoping I could go live with her and Baba. Instead, Nani says I must go far away where Aaie cannot find me. I'm scared and I don't want to go far away from my home. Nani wraps me in a rug. She puts the rug with me in it over her shoulder and walks a great distance with me.

After we are away from our village, and in the city, Nani gets me out. She then takes me to another city. Here we meet with a friend of Nani. She tells them what has happened and they tell her of a children's home that will take girls in to care for them. It is a Christian home and Nani agrees to take me there with her friend and see if she thinks it is safe for me. We travel some more to another city. I'm brought to New Beginnings Children's Home. There are boys and girls in this home. Nani meets with the home parents and we eat a meal with the children. Nani is concerned with me learning Christianity as we are Hindu's. Finally, she decides this is best because Aaie will never find me this far away. She tells me she will try to come visit me and can write to me too. She tells me the food is good and the children look well cared for and that I will be able to go to school here too. I have never been to school. I am not to write her or try to visit her. She then leaves me too.

In just a few weeks, I have lost my sisters, Baba, Aaie, Nana, and Nani. I miss my sisters so much and I cry for them. I can still see Chandani playing in her favorite red dress. It makes me cry even harder. I miss her so much it hurts. I do not speak of these things at the children's home. I am scared and all alone now.

Age Twelve

I am now in Standard Five at the government school the children at New Beginnings Children's Home attend. I have many friends here and enjoy living here. At first, I was scared, but life here is much easier than when I lived with Aaie and Baba. I see Nani once a year when she comes to visit. I never leave the home to visit relatives at break like some of the other children do, but I don't mind. I am safe living here. The chores are easy here and I don't mind doing them. I also love to help look after the younger girls in the home. I help them with bathing, dressing, doing their chores, and homework. I think of the sisters I lost and miss them. I think helping with the younger girls here helps me not miss them as much. I want to be a good example to the younger girls. I still love to play kho kho, but I also love pillow fights. I am always starting pillow fights with the girls that share my pink room.

When Nani visited with me last year, I learned that Baba had died. I see she is very sad and I tell her I remember him showing me the game of cricket. I ask what has happened to Aaie. She tells me that Aaie is a prostitute and a drunkard. She was very sad, but was glad to see me so big and learning so much. I read to her in English, which is my favorite class. I also shared stories from the Bible with her and told her about Jesus. Jesus is my father and mother now.

Leena during morning calisthenics in her favorite pink dress

Leena dancing in the play yard with one of the younger girls

About meeting Leena

One of the first things we noticed about Leena was her infectious smile. Leena is always smiling and has a bounce to her step. She truly is a sweet and engaging girl. She tried to answer all of our questions in English since it's her desire to be an English teacher when she grows up. Every day when the girls were playing in the yard of the home, Leena could be found making mud pies with the younger girls. Every day we were asked to take a taste of their pie. We always politely declined as Leena laughed and smiled. I got into a wild pillow fight with her and the girls, and played several games of kho kho – which we would say Leena dominated. She truly seems to enjoy life.

We talked with Leena many times and we knew from the house parents that her sisters were murdered by her mother. What no one knew was that Leena had witnessed the murders. As she told the story of her sisters' murders and what happened that night, she talked faster and faster, breathing very hard. It helped explain to the staff the nightmares she suffers from. We discussed her fear of her mother finding her and taking her away from the home. As she sat with us making a bracelet we were able to get her calmed down and smiling again. I am so thankful that Jesus gave us the right words to tell her that she was safe now and to share with her the belief that her sisters are with Jesus now too.

As we traveled through India, we were troubled by what had been shared regarding the murder of these three girls, coupled with what the staff shared about murder being a big issue in India. One of the many issues facing girls in India is feticide. As horrific as this event was, we hoped it was an isolated incident. Sadly, though, as we read the newspapers in each town we traveled through, we read story after story about girls being killed around their birth or aborted. On the television news, we saw similar reports, but we also saw a ray of hope. An obstetrician was trying to help. He said that he delivered nine boys for every one girl in his practice and that there would be sadness in the room when girls were born. He would like to change this by offering his patients money to help relieve the financial burden when they deliver girls. He stated that the gods also bless us with girl children, not just with boy children. In many cities, we saw billboards that said: "Save the Girl Child."

When we came home, we did more research and found the following facts about the continuing decline in the birth ratios of girls. In an article titled, "Girl Sex Ratio Declines," published in an Indian newspaper named, *The Hindu*, on June 12, 2013, we read: "The Karimnagar district attained a dubious distinction in the State with adverse girl child sex ratio of 920 girls for 1,000 boys against the State average of 935 for 1,000. Ironically, in some mandals, the girl sex ratio is even lower with below 800 girls for 1,000 boys."

We need to understand that there are many issues facing girl children in India, but according to UNICEF, the greatest issue is feticide.[9] The dowry is a major contributor to this problem as a bride's family is to bring the grooms family money, or a dowry, for marrying their son. This is a burden on many families to pay the dowry. Legislation has been passed by the Indian government making the practice of dowries and feticide illegal. It appears that the people are not following the law, or the law is not being enforced.

Despite her memories and being haunted by her sisters' murders, making her afraid of her mom finding her, Leena is happy at New Beginnings Children's Home. She is thriving, and spoke with us about wanting to be an English teacher and how someday she would like to do something for Jesus. She said Jesus saved her and she wants to serve Him. I asked her what the difference is between the Hindu and Christian religions, and she shared, "There is no hope in Hindu. In Christian there is hope. Whenever I lose hope, I sing Christian music and read scripture in the Bible."

9 Gupta, Alka. "Female feticide in India" *UNICEF:* http://www.unicef.org/india/media_3285.htm

Leena playing kho kho

Leena helping Pari with the wash

Leena singing during worship

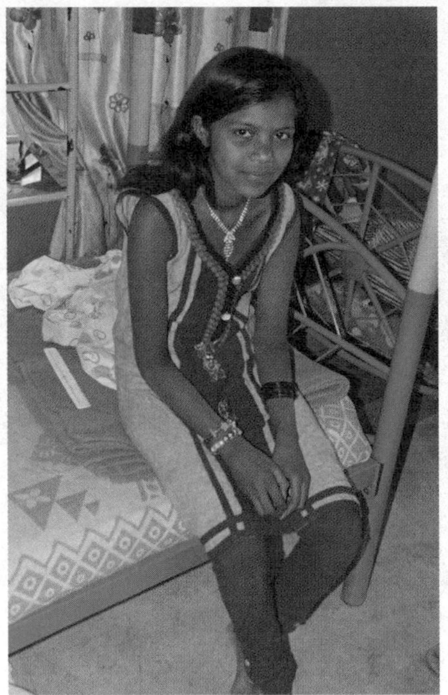

Leena showing us her bed at New Beginnings Children's Home

Leena having fun with the parachute

Leena praying during morning devotions

Deepak

Age Six

My name is Deepak and I am the youngest child in my family. I live with Baba who is a carpenter, Aaie who works making chapati, and my older brother, Samir, who is ten years old. I have an older sister, Parvani, who is sixteen years old. She is married and lives near us with her husband's family. We live in a very nice house with a stream of water. My family is Hindu and we worship different gods throughout the year.

I am starting school this year and am excited to go with my brother. My sister has not gone to school since she got married when she was fifteen. She now works scrubbing pots and pans, then helps take care of her husband's family. She has many chores. My brother and I like to play cricket and have many friends in our village. I enjoy spending time with my brother.

Aaie takes good care of us and is a very good cook. Baba is not around too much. He spends his time working and then likes to drink with his friends. Sometimes he drinks too much.

Age Seven

I have been in school for one year now and I like it very much. Standard Two is a lot of work but I don't mind. My favorite thing to study is Math. Samir is very smart and gets good grades in school. Samir is in Standard Six. After school we love to play cricket with our friends.

Baba has been sick and Aaie is worried. Parvani came over and Aaie was telling her Baba's liver has problems from all the drinking. His skin and eyes are yellow, he is sick to his stomach, and coughs up blood. He is not going to work now and Aaie wants Samir to go to work at a truck yard. She is talking with the truck driver who lives across the street from us about helping around the truck yard.

Baba is getting worse and Aaie is taking Samir to work for the truck yard. He doesn't want to leave school to go work, but there is no choice. Samir will work at the truck yard and the owner will pay Aaie 100 rupees a month for his work. Samir is leaving Standard Six, but maybe when Baba is better he can go back to school.

I am not sure Baba is going to get better. He never wakes up and Aaie is crying. We have very little money. Samir hates working at the truck yard. He is gone for days at a time traveling with the truck drivers. He works all over the country. He comes back angry and does not want to talk about his work. The truck owner gives the money he makes to Aaie, but Samir makes other money at the truck yard that they pay directly to him. He does not give this money to us. He spends it playing cards and other games at the truck yard.

Age Eight

Baba died a few weeks before I turned eight. Aaie is very upset and she is scared for us. She does not earn much money as a chapati maker. Parvani can't help us. Her money goes to her husband. Samir still works at the truck yard and I am to go to work there too. I will work on the truck with our neighbor. I will be his truck boy. I would rather go to school. Samir and I never play cricket anymore. He spends his time playing games at the truck yard. Sometimes I smell alcohol on him when he comes home.

The truck driver, Aamir, tells me to be careful and not stay at the truck yard in the evening. He says bad things happen to the boys after work at the yard. I am to stay close to him and he will take me to and from work. As he tells me this I think of Samir and how he spends his time at the truck yard. I hope no bad things are happening to him, but I think maybe they are. He has changed.

Aaie tells me it is important we all work now. I hope we can make enough to keep our house. It is a good strong house, my Baba built it with his carpenter skills. I love our house and never want to leave. I decide to work hard for Aamir to earn my 100 rupees a month from the truck owner. My job on the truck is to help keep it clean. I help wash the truck and clean all the windows. When we stop, I make sure the windows stay clean. Aamir is very nice to me and always shares his food with me. He likes to eat egg curry and rice. We start work at 5:30 a.m. and end at 8:00 p.m. We travel long distances delivering many different things attached to our cab.

My favorite thing to deliver is Bobcat tractors. We have a special bed attached to the cab and load it with two layers of tractors to deliver. On these trips, I like to sit on the top row of tractors instead of in the cab. I like to feel the wind from up there. When I am not riding up on the tractors, and I'm in the cab with Aamir, he tells me many different things. He shares his Muslim faith with me and tells me all things about his family. He makes sure I go home at night to Aaie. He is very concerned about the things my brother is involved in at the truck yard. The truck yard owner pays Aaie 200 rupees a month for Samir and my work. Aamir sometimes pays me extra that I can use when we travel for food and drink. He is a very good man.

Age Nine

Aamir and I travel all over western India and I am a very good navigator. He tells me how to drive the truck, but I am too small to drive right now. Someday, maybe I will be a truck driver like Aamir. He tells me I am a very good navigator and he can trust my memory on directions as we travel to different cities. I keep the truck cab very clean and always make sure the windows are cleaned too whenever we stop. I start to like not going to school, and on Sundays I play cricket with my friends. Samir does not play cricket anymore, he prefers to hang out at the truck yard. I have much freedom and I like not having too many rules to follow.

Aamir and I just got back from a two-day run. When I get home, Aaie is not there and Samir tells me that she is dead. Parvani tells me Aaie was hit by a car walking home from work. It is decided I am to try to live with Parvani, and her husband, Sai. I want to stay in my house with Samir. He is thirteen and I want to stay here in my home. Aamir is talking with us now, too, and he thinks I should go with my sister. He will pick me up there for work. Parvani talks with the truck yard owner and arranges for another time for me to work for him. She and Sai will now get the money for my work.

Sai does not like me living in their home. He is constantly complaining about me. Parvani tries to point out I am bringing 100 rupees a month into their home to help. That I am on the road much of the time, but he still does not like me living with them. I never see Samir except in the truck yard. He is drinking alcohol and any money he gets, he gambles away. I'm worried we will lose our house and wish I was living there with Samir to make sure the house is all right. I think about Aaie and how hard it was for us after Baba died. I miss Aaie and her good cooking.

Deepak worked on a truck like this one

I have lived with Parvani for three months and now I must leave. I can't go to my house because Samir lost the house gambling. He gambled away our home. I am very mad at Samir. He is just like Baba with alcohol. Things are very bad for us. I tell Aamir all my trouble and he says I can live in the truck cab. He does not want me staying at the truck yard. Over time, I listen to the older boys tell me that there are good things for me to do and make money at the truck yard. With Aaie gone, I decide to see what happens at the truck yard and I decide to stay there one weekend instead of sleeping in the truck cab.

Deepak at New Beginnings Children's Home

The older boys give me alcohol to drink and it makes me sick. They say I will get used to it over time. There are card and dice games going on around the yard. In one place, the men watch bad movies. The truck yard owner is glad to see me there and tells me this is a way I can earn more money for myself. I'm given odd jobs to do all weekend. I help with the gambling games, clean the toilets, office, and garbage drains. I talked to the truck yard owner who told me this was my life now. He said that there was nothing better for me. At the end of the weekend, he gave me twenty rupees.

Aamir was upset that I was starting to work at the truck yard and stay there. He kept warning me that there are many bad influences at the truck yard and that I needed to be careful or bad things could happen to me. Since I could not stay with Parvani, even though they get 100 rupees a month for me working at the truck yard, I decided to stay at the truck yard to earn my own money.

Age Ten

Samir and his friends run the younger boys at the truck yard. I now run some of the gambling and usually drink alcohol. One night some of the older boys take me and we drink a lot of alcohol. They tell me they are going to help me earn big money tonight. They tell me I am going to go with them and I am to do what I am told and will get paid very well. I am so drunk. They take me to a group of five men. They take my pants down and hold me down as each man does horrible things with me. Afterwards, they make fun of me and call me horrible things. Then they take the money they got from the men and give me nothing.

Aamir was right, horrible things happen at the truck yard. These horrible things now happen regularly and I do not know what to do. I have nowhere to go. One of the boys I am friends with disappears one night and the older boys tell me if I don't want to disappear too, I had better do as they tell me. The truck yard owner tells me this is my life and all that I am ever going to be. He says, "There is nowhere for you to go and no one that wants you."

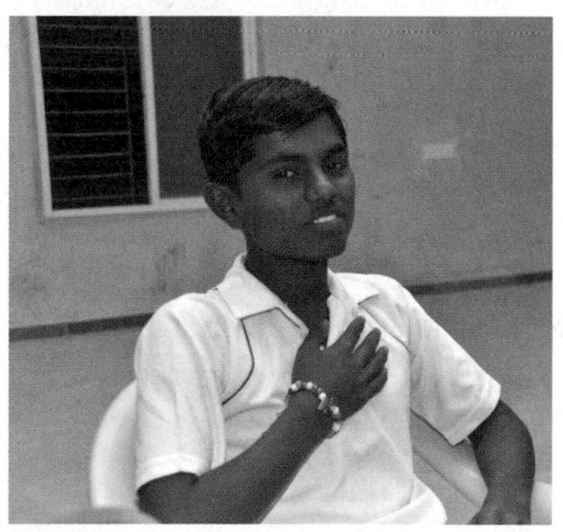

Deepak sharing his story with us

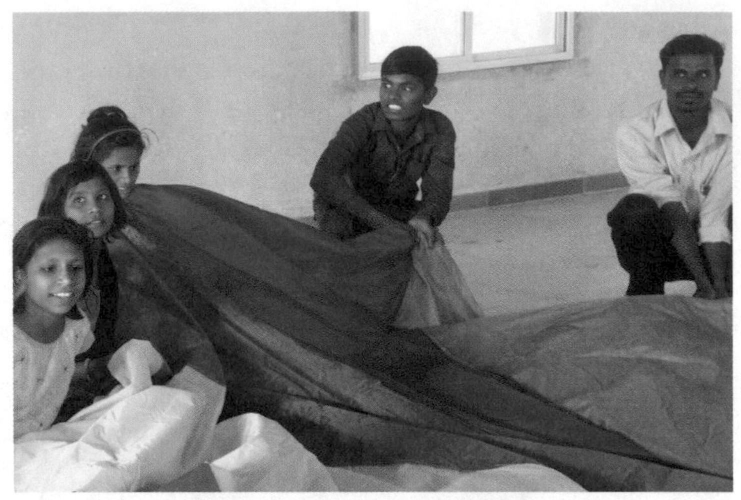

Getting ready for a parachute game

I try again to live with Parvani and Sai, but it makes Sai angry to have me living with them again. He now beats my sister and she says it is worse now that I am living with them. She asks me to please leave. They get 100 rupees for giving me to the truck yard to work but I am not welcome in their home. Samir laughs at me and tells me to grow up when I try to talk with him. My beautiful home is gone and I can hardly look Aamir in the eyes. I am so ashamed of what I have become.

Age Twelve

I am back living in the truck and trying to stay away from the truck yard as much as possible. Aamir and I are leaving on a long haul. I breakdown as we travel and I tell him everything that has happened to me. He tells me that I need to get out of there and go back to school. We talk about any relatives I may have that he could take me to for help. Aamir says I am very brave to share these things with him for help. He does not seem mad at me but at the truck yard owner.

Aamir says the truck yard owner is a bad man that earns

money off of sex and gambling of the truckers and truck boys. He has heard of other illegal things like boys being sold for their kidneys or other indentured work to cover gambling debts. He and I discuss going to talk with my aunt in another city to see if she could help me. I have a very good memory and only need to go somewhere once and remember where it is. I know exactly how to get to my aunts' house because I have gone there twice. Aamir takes me there when our work is done. He talks with her for a long time. She takes me in and says she knows of a place that will take boys like me to help them. She says at this place I will go to school and be well cared for by the people.

Aamir and I say good bye. He tells me to be strong and finish school. I will miss Aamir, he has always been nice to me. My aunt arranges for me to go to a place called New Beginnings Children's Home. We visit the home, and there are boys and girls living there. They have food, clothes, games, and all go to school. I am not sure I will like living here in a Christian home. There are many rules that are explained to me. My aunt tells me goodbye and that I can come to her house on breaks. She tells me I will do well here. She knows of a boy that came from here and he has done very well.

After a week, I run away from New Beginnings Children's Home. I can't stand all the rules at the home or the school. I am used to being free. I miss Aamir and the open road. I do not miss the truck yard and truck owner. After roaming for a few days and trash picking I return to New Beginnings Children's Home. I am surprised the staff welcome me back with open arms. They encourage me to follow the rules. We get up at 5:00 a.m. every day to do exercises. We then clean up our bedrolls and get dressed for school. Next, we have devotion and prayer time, eat breakfast, then go to school. There are more rules at school and I have trouble sitting in class. I am also in class with younger kids. I am twelve and in Standard Three.

Deepak cleaning

Deepak playing with a dog

In week two I run away again. I just want to feel free. This time I stay away for a week just roaming the city. I beg and trash pick. Finally, I decide to go back again. Once again, they welcome me with open arms. They talk with me again about what is troubling me and causing me to run. I tell them the chores are not hard, it's the rules – I am not used to all of these rules. We discuss this, but I can't explain what's hard, other than just having rules. There are rules at the home and more rules at school. I do enjoy recess at school, and all the games we play at the home. There is plenty of time for playing cricket.

I have nightmares at night, and I wake up shaking and sick to my stomach. I think of the horrible things the men did to me. I don't share any of what happened to me with the other children or house parents at the home. After a month, I run away again. After a couple of days, I return hungry and scared. Once again, I'm surprised that I'm welcomed back with open arms. They seem to have really missed me and are glad I am back. I am allowed to get cleaned up and put on clean clothes. Then they fix me a meal and ask how they can help me.

I tell them I don't understand why they welcome me back when I run away. The house father tells me about the Prodigal Son in the Bible. He said I will always be welcome and he hopes I come to see that this is where it is good for me. He is praying that I will see that Jesus loves me and God wants me here in this home. I will always be welcome here. He says I will be safe here.

Age Fifteen

Three years now I have lived at New Beginnings Children's Home. I have worked hard in school and have moved to be in Standard Seven. Math is still my favorite subject. Cricket and Frisbee are my favorite games. I have grown quite a bit while I have been here at the home.

I am a leader of the boys and have many responsibilities. I

lead the boys in calisthenics and their chores. I help them get ready for the day and with their studies. I tell them it is safe here and there are many bad things in the world. That they are blessed to be in this home. I teach them Christian songs and Bible verses. I love to read about John the Baptist and of the Prodigal Son. I share how I have forgotten many bad things now that I am a new person in the Lord.

Deepak leading the boys in morning calisthenics

Deepak eating dinner

About meeting Deepak

Deepak was an engaging, hardworking teenager. He was assigned to help us at the home and he was constantly attentive to what we were doing. His understanding of the English language was not very good, but somehow we always understood each other. He had the most beautiful smile that started our days, bright and early, at 5:00 a.m. He insisted we join the boys outside our room for morning calisthenics. He would wait patiently while we tried to bend this way and that, holding each pose until we achieved it properly. He openly cared for the young boys in his room of the home. I noticed him checking that they were groomed or ready for school on numerous occasions.

Although he was a "cool" fifteen, when it came to game time, he laughed and played like a child. He really loved cricket, and when we came back to the home with new cricket supplies from one of our donors, he was so excited he was actually jumping up and down with joy. Previously they played with a board and ball.

When he shared the abuse he suffered as a truck boy it was painful. We told him he did not need to relive the painful memories because we could see it was making him physically ill. He said, "No. No I must tell." He talked late into the night telling of sexual abuse after sexual abuse, needing to purge each incident. Then he shared how he still has nightmares that they are coming to get him and take him back. He was shaking with a headache and stomach ache by the time he finished. We wrapped him in a blanket and prayed with him until his breathing and heart slowed down. He kept telling us he is now with good men and it is over. The house parents at New Beginnings Children's Home had not been told by Deepak's aunt the abuse he had suffered. They thought he had just been beaten and verbally abused. It was so bad, everyone in the room felt ill just hearing of the atrocities inflicted on this young boy.

Fortunately, due to the good men at the home, Deepak was

back to himself the next afternoon. They talked with him about how he could come to them when he had nightmares, and they would pray with him for Jesus to take them away. They told him he is a new person in Jesus, and the men who did these things were bad, not Deepak. Deepak is a very good and brave man.

Our last meeting with Deepak was good. He shared a picture he had drawn for us of his house. He still, to this day, wishes he could have his house back. He even asked if there was a way we could buy his house for him to have when he grows up.

Deepak loves to eat chapati, worship God, and hear God's story. His favorite color is sky blue. He is a wonderful young man with a hope and a future. He wants to go to the police academy to be a police officer. When we asked him why he wanted to be a police officer, he quickly responded, to arrest the bad men who hurt children.

Deepak's picture of the home he grew up in as a small boy

Deepak hanging out with one of the house parents

Deepak showing us a hand stand

Deepak praying during morning devotions

Shanta

Age Five

Aaie is dead. Baba is telling me that I must tell the police my Aunty killed Aaie, that my Aunty poisoned her. He wants me to say I saw Aunty put fertilizer in Aaie's water. I didn't see anything. I am scared and don't understand what is going on. The police come to talk with us. While the police talk with Baba, my uncle tells me to tell the police Baba poisoned Aaie. Uncle is very angry. I hear the police asking who put the poison in the water Aaie drank. I don't understand why anyone would poison Aaie. I am so scared I don't speak when the police try to talk with me. Aunty keeps crying out, "My sister died, my sister died, my sister died!" She is so distraught she does not speak to the police either. Nani is now here too, and she tells the police that her son did not do this thing.

Baba is being taken away by the police. Uncle and Nani are arguing. My little brother, Veer, is still sleeping. I can't believe he is not awake and crying. I think everyone has forgotten about us as they argue. I sit and listen to them yelling about who poisoned Aaie. Nani gets Veer and tells me to come with her. Uncle is yelling about Baba murdering his sister and saying we all carry the blood of a murderer. Nani walks very fast and we leave everything behind as we leave. I just keep walking and don't say a word. I think about Baba, and how if I told the police what he told me to say, then the police would not have taken him away. Nani is crying as we walk. Veer is crying. I am crying too.

At Nani's house she feeds Veer and he goes back to sleep. I can't eat. I am so scared and want my Aaie. Nani asks me what I saw. I told her I didn't see anything. When I came in from playing, Aaie was laying down and everyone said she was dead. I told her that Baba told me that Aunty gave her poison fertilizer. Nani is very worried. We sit for a long time not talking. I'm scared and don't know what will happen to Veer and me. I miss my Aaie and Baba. I am very scared and don't understand what has happened.

Veer is only two months old and Nani takes good care of him. We don't have much food and we can't get help. People talk of us as if we're murderers. I don't know who killed Aaie, but I know I didn't, and neither did Nani, or Veer. We didn't get to go to Aaie's funeral fire. I don't know where her ashes were spread. Nani tells me it is dangerous to be around Uncle and Aunty. She's heard they are threatening revenge for their sister's death. I go begging almost every day to get money for us. I pass a temple each day and the Buddhist monks are nice to me and sometimes give me food to eat.

We had just put Veer down to sleep when I heard a commotion outside of our hut. Uncle and a group of men are coming towards our hut yelling. They say, "Child of murderer!" and, "You carry the blood of a killer." Nani puts things around Veer to hide him and tells me to run to the temple for protection. To keep the men from following me, Nani runs out the back and into the fields. I start to run to the huts near us, but I'm afraid to leave Veer. I look back and see that my uncles have stones and so do the men with them. It looks like they want to stone us to death. The people in the hut near us will not help me, so I keep going until I get to the temple. The monks let me hide in the temple. I'm told to stay there overnight where I am safe. I wish Nani had taken Veer. I hope Veer is not found by the angry group. I lay down in the temple on a blanket that the monks give me. They offer me food but I'm too upset to eat. I lay there crying.

Age Six

I just turned six and my little brother is now six months old. My uncles have not stopped looking for us, but they can't find us to stone us to death. They have come four times since Aaie was killed. Each time we've gotten away. I run to the temple and the Buddhist monks always hide me. It's been several months since they last came and I hope they have forgotten about us. I have nightmares about Aaie dying and about being stoned to death. I wonder what is happening to Baba in prison. Nani says he did not kill Aaie. It hurts my head as I think and think, but I do not know who would poison Aaie.

I help Nani take care of my brother when I am not at the temple or begging. Veer is a lot of work for Nani. I help bathe and feed him. I help with laundry and cooking too. Some days we have no food to eat. I go every day to the temple begging for money. I have to try to get money so we can have food. Nani is too old to work and she says I must help. I can always count on the monks to give me some food. I am careful to take food to Nani too.

When I am begging, people sometimes are not nice. They yell at me and called me names. Sometimes they push me away or hit me. I'm only trying to get money for us to live. Some people are nice and give me money. I don't like begging, and there are other kids there begging too. The most help I get is from the monks. They give clothes to Veer and me. They give me food almost every day. I feel safe when I am at the temple and know the monks look out to protect me.

Age Seven

I am seven years old now and Veer just turned two. He can walk now and sometimes I take him by the hand and bring him to the temple with me. He does not walk as well as me, but we get there and back. He plays while I beg, but he always stays close to me. The monks continue to help us with clothes and some food. Nani does some work cleaning pots and pans while I watch Veer to bring in more money for us. She hasn't been feeling well and I worry for her.

Nani is sick and cannot get up today to work. I worry about her but she tells me that I should take Veer and go to the temple to beg for money. We go, but I don't like leaving her this sick. It is a good day at the temple because the monks give us food. We got some money too from begging. We walk as fast as we can to get back to Nani, but Veer slows me down. He can't walk very fast.

Nani died today. We stayed at the hut because she was not feeling well and she died in her sleep. I could not wake her up. We went to the temple for help. The monks are taking care of Nani and sending chants for her to pass on from this life. They will handle her funeral fire and we are to go live at the temple. We cannot go to Aaie's family because it is well known they would kill us. After three days, Nani has a Buddhist funeral. There is a fire in which her body is burned. Then the ashes are thrown in a river near our village. Veer and I attend Nani's funeral along with Aunty who came for the funeral. She is Baba's sister. Aunty lives with her husband's family and says there is no room for us to come with her. Aunty insists she cannot take us and that we should stay with the monks. Veer and I take our blankets and few clothes to the temple. I don't like Aunty anyway, and I know the monks have always looked out for us.

Shanta and Veer

Age Nine

For almost two years, Veer and I have lived at the temple. We beg during the day to get extra money and are glad with how the monks look out for us. We get clothes and food from them. We also use the money we get from begging to get extra food. Veer does not remember Aaie, Baba, or Nani. I tell him stories about them. We don't have toys, but Veer and I play games. We sometimes play and fight with the other kids that beg at the temple and in the streets.

Buddhist Temple in India similar to where Shanta and Veer lived

At night we sleep together wrapped in a blanket. I put Veer against the wall and I sleep on the outside. I always let Veer eat first to make sure he gets enough food. I do my best to take good care of him. I wash our clothes and make sure we wash up too. We don't have shoes and only a couple things to wear, but somehow we make it each day. When we are begging, I make sure no one hurts Veer and I watch out for him. Sometimes we go through trash looking for things we can sell for money, but that is messy and I don't like doing it. I prefer we just beg.

Every day I see kids walking to school. They stop at the shops and buy bags of water or milk for school. They wear uniforms and carry their lunch buckets with them. I wonder what it would be like to go to school. They look so happy and don't have to beg like we do. I wonder if Aaie and Baba were with us if we too would go to school and have lunch buckets. I wonder what these kids do in school. I see them walk home at the end of the school day. The kids walk in groups, girls with girls, and boys with boys. They talk and laugh as they head home. I never see any of the uniform kids beg at the temple. I never see any of the kids begging at the temple go to school either.

Today an amazing thing happened. Baba came to the temple looking for us. I could not believe our Baba was here. Veer is scared of him. He was just a baby the last time we saw Baba, so he does not know who this man is. I tell Veer this is our Baba and he will now take care of us! I was filled with joy and tell Baba everything that has happened to us. When he hears about how our uncles tried to stone us to death, he gets very angry. He tells us to come with him. We walk back to Uncle's house where we used to live, and Baba and Uncle get in a fist fight. The police come and they take Baba, Veer, and me to the police station.

The police are not very nice to us. They lock Veer and me in a cell. Baba is not here with us and has been taken away. When he comes back his shirt is ripped and his back is bloody and bruised from being beaten. I ask Baba what happened, but he won't talk with me. We stay in the cell for three days and then we are released. Baba says we are going to another village to where Aunty lives with her husband. He says they will help us.

Veer with his friends at New Beginnings Children's Home

Shanta looking out of her bedroom window

Age Ten

We move into Aunty's house. She has two children of her own and Veer likes to play with them. I hear her and Baba talk about us and how he needs her to look after us while he searches for work. Aunty does not like having us, so I try to help. I watch all three younger kids. I help wash dishes and wash clothes. Sometimes, Aunty beats us for no reason. I hope we don't have to live here long.

Baba gets a job building wells. This means he must travel to where the work is being done. He says we are to live with Aunty and do as she asks. He says he will be back to visit us. When he comes back he tells us we are moving to live with him and his new wife. We leave Aunty's house to go live with Baba and his new wife.

Veer and I like living with Baba, but we don't like Baba's new wife. She is meaner than Aunty. Baba leaves for work for days at a time and we are left home. One day I make my step-mom very mad and she picks me up and throws me down on the ground. I am very sore and when Baba comes back, we learn that my collarbone was broken. It hurts very badly and I want to leave living here in this home. Baba gets in an argument with his wife.

Baba takes Veer and me back to live with Aunty. Baba tells us it is just until he gets things settled with his new wife. Aunty, I can tell, is not happy to have us back. We live in her home doing much work. The work is harder for me with my collarbone injured. I cannot lift my arm too high without pain. One day she tells us that she has arranged for us to go live in a home where we can go to school. She tells us at breaks we will come back to live with her and see Baba if he is in town. She said it's best for us to go to this school. She learned about it from other people in the village.

Veer is now five and I am going to turn eleven. I'm worried that Baba will not know where we are when we are at this school. We travel to another town with Aunty. She takes us to this place called New Beginnings Children's Home. I notice the kids are all wearing school uniforms and are playing. Some are playing pots and pans, others jump rope. The boys are playing cricket and Veer is very excited about this game. We meet the people who run the home and they talk with Aunty and us. We are assured that at breaks we will go to our Aunty's house. Aunty promises when Baba comes she will tell him where we are and that he is allowed to come here and visit with us.

I am happy right away to live here. We are taken to a doctor who looks at my collarbone and another doctor checks that we are healthy. We are given clean clothes and taken to meet teachers at the school. There is plenty of good food. We have chores, but they are not hard. Best of all, I have a bed of my own. Veer sleeps in a boy's room with other boys his age. He sleeps on a mattress on the floor, but the girls get to sleep in real beds, with pillows and sheets and blankets. I love my bed!

Shanta playing pots and pans

Shanta's picture of her church

Age Thirteen

For three school sessions we have lived at New Beginnings Children's Home. I do very well in school and am in Standard Four, Position One in my class. I enjoy school very much and my favorite subject is English. I want to be a doctor when I finish school so that I can serve the poor and the needy. Veer is in Standard Three in school. His favorite subject is Math. He and I love living here. The work is easy, the food is good, and there is plenty of time to play. I love to play pots and pans. I also like to jump rope, but it is hard, and sometimes hurts my collarbone. We don't like break time when we have to go stay at Aunty's house. There the work is hard and we eat very little food. Veer and I would rather stay at New Beginnings Children's Home, but we go hoping to see Baba. He is never there and Aunty says he is a drunk and off digging wells.

Since coming to New Beginnings Children's Home I have become a Christian. We have daily Bible study with our house parents. They teach us stories from the Bible. We also work on memorizing Scripture. My favorite thing is to sing worship songs. We start and end devotion time with worship songs. My favorite song is *I will fly with Jesus.*

Shanta carrying one of the younger girls

Veer blowing bubbles

About meeting Shanta

Shanta is a strong young woman. She is very serious in her studies and work. She does like to play, but there is always a seriousness to her play. Having to care for herself and her brother, from such a young age, has caused her to seem and act older than other girls her age. I noticed she went about her chores with a robust gusto. She can frequently be found looking after Veer. He shared with me that she helps him bathe, wash his clothes, do his homework, and makes sure he behaves. He said she teaches him to treat others nice.

Veer is more age appropriate than Shanta. It is apparent that she took very good care of him throughout all of the difficulty they've gone through. She was definitely the strong one during all of their trials. Veer's memories started with Shanta and him living at the temple. He remembers sleeping, wrapped up with her body and a blanket. He shared how she always made sure he was fed and protected him in fights with other kids. He remembered her telling him the man he did not know was his father. He also goes to Aunty's house hoping to see his father. He said he would rather stay at the home at break. He does not like it at Aunty's house.

We take pictures of the children as they are going about their day for this book and Shanta loved having her picture taken. She would follow us around whenever the camera was out, and always wanted to see the photo. Then when we showed her the photo she was surprised to see herself in the photo and laughed, showing everyone around the photo.

Both children spoke openly about their Christian beliefs. Shanta wanted to have us record her singing, *I will fly with Jesus*. In typical Shanta style, she watched the video to see herself. We asked Shanta what the difference is between being a Buddhist and a Christian. She responded, "Jesus is the living God and Buddhists worship idols."

Shanta and Veer trying to figure out a Rubik's Cube

Shanta coloring her picture

Shanta dancing

Shanta with her friends

Trisha

Age Seven

I am Trisha and I live in the Dhavari Slum in Mumbai with my family. There are seven of us in my family – Baba, Aaie, my older brother Amogh, eleven, my older sister Shreya, nine, my younger sister Rani, five, and my youngest brother Kishan, three. We all live in a one room, tin roof shack. It is crowded, but Aaie takes very good care of us. She makes sure to keep us safe. She makes sure my older brother and sister go to the government school. Surrounding our slum are beautiful hotels. We live on the airport property. The ladies and Aaie talk about this when we are getting water or waiting in line to go to the bathrooms we share at the end of our slum. The lines at the bathroom are very long. The bathroom is near one of the places the airplanes land and I like to watch the airplanes land.

My Baba works as a construction worker. Aaie does not work anymore, she takes care of us children. Baba gets upset with Aaie for not working. He would like her to leave us and get back to construction work. They fight about this, but she will not leave her children alone. Baba thinks Shreya could stay home and watch us. Aaie tells Baba that education for her children is their hope. I am in school this year, too, with Shreya and Amogh. Aaie got us signed up into the government school. She makes sure we go to school very clean. We are not to play or work in our school clothes. I like school very much and pay attention to the teacher. Some days the teacher does not do much with us, but I stay and wait, because some days she does.

I help with chores at home. Aaie shows me how to do laundry, make chapatti, and wash my younger sister and brother. Shreya, Rani, and I love to play pots and pans. We make little fires and boil water with anything we can find. We pretend we are making soup. We also make mud pies. Shreya likes for us to play kho kho with other kids outside. My brother Amogh likes to play cricket. Aaie is always keeping a close eye on us. Aaie likes to sing and dance with us. She shows me dance moves and I think she is beautiful. I like to dance best of all. We all sleep together in our one room on blankets.

Baba does not play with us. He works all day and then in the evening he goes out drinking and gambling. Aaie and he fight over the drinking and gambling. I don't mind it when Baba is out, then Aaie is happier. They fight too much, especially when Baba has had too much to drink. Sometimes there is no money for food. We go some days with nothing to eat. Amogh and Shreya will go out, before and after school sometimes, trash picking to try and get extra money for us. Aaie does not like us to trash pick. She says it is not safe. Sometimes, Aaie talks to us about life in the village before Baba and her moved here to Mumbai. She said there was no work for them in the village and they came here to work construction. Now she thinks things were maybe better in the village.

Age Eight

Baba and Aaie are fighting again. Kishan, Rani, and Amogh are not home. Shreya and I were helping Aaie cook dinner when Baba came home drunk. The fight is bad and Aaie is not backing down. She is yelling at Baba for drinking and taking food from their children. Baba has her backed against the shack wall and is yelling that he will do what he pleases. Shreya and I are against the opposite wall not moving. I hope Baba doesn't hit Aaie. I can't stand it when he hits her, or us. He scares me when he is this mad and drunk.

The fight is not ending and Baba is saying he should just kill Aaie. Aaie yells at him to go ahead and do it, and end this life. Baba picks up the cooking gas, and says he'll throw it on her, and burn her to death. Aaie is yelling back at him. Shreya and I are not moving. We both know this fight is the worst one we've ever seen. Baba takes the cooking gas and throws it all over Aaie. Aaie puts her arms over her face and starts yelling for help. Baba takes a match and lights it. Baba holds the match, yelling, "Is this what you want, for me to end this miserable life?" I can't scream or move. Shreya is shaking next to me. It happened so fast but almost in slow motion at the same time. The match went from Baba's hand and lit Aaie on fire. She ran screaming on fire out of our shack as the fire spread all over her. Aaie was screaming, "Please save me, please save me, please save me!" She lay in the street on fire as people gathered around watching. She was rolled until the fire was out. She was burned all over and I could hardly recognize Aaie. The smell was awful. Someone ran for help.

Baba told us, over and over, that we were to tell the police it was a cooking accident. He kept saying Aaie made him do this horrible thing, and we must say it was a cooking accident. Then Baba went and was talking to Aaie in the street. The police came and Aaie was taken to the hospital burn unit. Baba took Shreya and me with him to the hospital. We waited a long time to see a doctor. The doctor told Baba that Aaie had burns over 90% of her body. He asked how this happened as Aaie would not say. Baba said it was a cooking accident. Shreya and I stayed quiet. We were finally allowed to see Aaie. She had tubes all over her and was covered. She could barely talk and I don't think she even knew we were there. I heard Baba telling her that she had better say it was an accident to save her daughters.

The police came to the hospital and Aaie told them it was a cooking accident. Shreya and I did not talk to the police. We sat on the floor by Aaie's bed crying softly. It was determined we were too upset to talk since we had been helping Aaie cook. Once the police left, Baba took us home. He told Kishan, Rani and Amogh that Aaie had an accident while cooking. Baba lied and said that it was just a horrible accident. He told them she was in the hospital and that the next day we would go see how Aaie was doing. Shreya and I went to our shrine to make a coconut offering to the Hindu god Ganesh. We prayed to god Ganesh to save Aaie. Shreya cried as she was praying. The next two days we spent between the hospital and home. We sat at Aaie's bedside with no way to help her. Then we would go home and give offerings to god Ganesh. We gave god Ganesh coconuts, flowers and burned incense. We kept a constant focus on asking god Ganesh to help Aaie.

Our beautiful Aaie is gone. The doctor tells Baba the burns were too bad and they could not save her. I don't know what will happen to us now. I feel so empty and sad. I sit in our home trying to talk with Shreya. She says we will not speak of Aaie and that I should go to sleep. Baba is out drinking with his friends. Amogh is out too. Rani, Kishan, and I lay down as Shreya tells us to. I finally fall asleep but wake up from a nightmare of Aaie's burning. In my dream I hear her screaming over and over again for help.

Shreya, Trisha, Kisahn and Rani

Much loved and cried over picture of Trisha's Mom

Amogh, Shreya, and I don't go back to school. Baba wants Amogh to start working at the construction site. Shreya, Rani, Kishan, and I are to trash pick and look after each other. I miss Aaie very much. Shreya tries very hard to take care of us and replace Aaie. She cooks and washes us. I help with laundry. We all stick together while we trash pick. It is hard and dirty work and I see why Aaie did not want us to do this work. It makes me think that she loved us very much. There are so many people from the slums also picking trash, that it is hard. We work from morning to evening and make very little money for food. Shreya keeps us together as we work and uses our money to buy whatever food she can. Baba is gone drinking almost every night. Sometimes we don't even see him.

The nights are the worst time for me. I am very scared and have nightmares of Aaie burning to death. I hear her screams, over and over again. I wake up shaking and crying several times a night. I don't like to sleep anymore. Sometimes the dreams turn to me being burned to death. I feel the cooking gas pouring on me and see the match coming to light me on fire. Shreya comforts me and talks quietly to me. She tells me we will be all right. It was just a horrible accident. I know different.

Age Nine

It is a hard life for us in the slums of Mumbai. Kishan is leaving us to live in a boy's home. A pastor has convinced Baba that Kishan will be educated and fed in the home. He will have a chance to be an educated man. The boy's home is here in Mumbai and Baba can visit Kishan. He also tells him of a place in another part of India with a home that takes girls, and gives them an education and food. The pastor comes through our slum several times a week. He knows that we are starving and competing with many other trash pickers. The pastor is kind to us, and brings us food and clothes when he can.

Baba and Amogh only find work sometimes. They drink alcohol and gamble most of what they make. Since Aaie's death, Baba is drinking more often. He sometimes is not at the construction site but out drinking. Shreya tells me we must never say anything about Baba drinking alcohol and gambling. We are to stay quiet and try to take care of ourselves. Life keeps getting harder and it has not been a year yet since Aaie died.

It is decided that Kishan is going to live in the boy's home here in Mumbai. I am glad that he will have food, clothes, and get to go to school. I also know that we will miss him. Kishan, Shreya, Rani, and I all have worked together for the last few months since Aaie died to try to save ourselves from starving to death. I hope Kishan will be fed well and go to a good school where he will be treated well.

Rani helping with food preparation

Kishan eating breakfast before school

Baba and the pastor are ready to leave. Kishan was scared but went with them. Shreya tells Kishan that he will be fine and that she trusts Pastor. He has only tried to help us. With Kishan gone, there is one less mouth to feed in our family. Shreya talks with Pastor the next time he comes about us girls going to the home he told Baba about. Pastor tells her it is a very nice home and we would have clothes, plenty of food, and we'd go to school. Shreya asks Pastor to talk with Baba to see if we can also move to the home. I tell Shreya that I'm scared to go to another town and wonder how we'll ever see Kishan again if we're far away. Shreya tells us it is better if we go to the girl's home with Aaie gone and Baba off drinking. Shreya misses going to school and tells us she hopes that Baba will let us go because it will be for the best.

Baba has decided to let us move to the girl's home. It is a long train ride from Mumbai to our new home. Pastor and Baba take us to New Beginnings Children's Home. I like it right away. Shreya and Rani also like it right away. We are introduced to many children. There are also boys here, and I wish Kishan could come here too. Shreya and I ask Baba if Kishan could come here to be with us. He said that he could not because he wanted to keep Kishan close to him in Mumbai. Baba and Pastor don't stay for long after the paperwork is done and Baba sees we're taken care of. He quickly leaves to go back to Mumbai.

After he left, we were fed a great meal and had second helpings of food. We then were shown our room. The walls were bright colors and we had our own beds, pillows and blankets. My room was bigger than our whole shack in the slum. I loved my bed. We were shown our showers, how to brush our teeth, and given clothes and shoes.

The next day we were taken to a doctor to get a checkup. The doctor said that Shreya needed glasses so she could see better. The home paid to have glasses made for her to see well again. We were also taken to get set up to start school. The school was very crowded and I was a little nervous about starting school again.

Back at the home we were given chores to do to help. I had to sweep the rooms and help some in the kitchen. Mostly we played with the other kids. We played pots and pans, kho kho, and learned some new dance games. At night, in my bed though, the nightmares are still coming. I wake up shaking and screaming. The home parents come and ask me what my nightmare is about. I am afraid to talk. Shreya says we are not to talk about Aaie.

Age Ten

I have been at New Beginnings Children's Home for over a year. I am so happy here and the nightmares rarely happen now. I have not seen Baba since he left here. He said he would come visit us but he has not. Shreya, Rani, and I stay here at the home year-round. Most of the kids leave on school break to visit any relatives they have. We don't have anywhere to go, but Shreya still takes good care of us. She helps us with laundry, bathing, playing, and most of all, with our homework. Shreya is very smart and is in Position One in school. She wants to be a nurse someday to help people in the hospital get better. I think she will be a good nurse. I want to be a dancer when I grow up. I love to dance and remember Aaie teaching me how to dance.

Trisha during one of her interviews with us

Today we got a surprise. The house parents told us that Baba and Kishan were coming to visit us. They said that Kishan may stay here at the home with us. He has had an accident at the home in Mumbai that has left him blind in one eye. I can hardly believe that Kishan is coming here. Shreya is very concerned about his injury. She says it is good that he comes here because we get very good medical care at this home. Kishan's left eye is messed up bad. A boy at the school accidently hit him in the eye with a stick. Baba is very upset for Kishan and brought him here to get medical treatment. Baba says we look good and are growing up. He stays for a day and visits with us. We learn that Amogh does not work construction anymore. He works the boards for bands. We tell Baba about our school and what we have learned about Jesus. Shreya tells him he should talk with Pastor in Mumbai. He left us again to go back to Mumbai to work. He tells us he will come back and visit us again. We wonder if he will because he has not come to visit us before.

Shreya coming to help us with translation

Kishan gets drops from the doctor for his eye. It waters all the time. We are sad because the doctor told us he cannot fix Kishan's eye. He will never see out of the eye again. It is odd, but Kishan does not mind. He is glad to be with us again. He tells us this home is nicer than the home in Mumbai. He really likes it here and makes friends with the other boys quickly. Kishan likes to play cricket and pray to God. Kishan tells us he loves Jesus and that Jesus is both his Aaie and Baba. He said that Jesus looks out for him, and brought him to be with us in this beautiful home. He tells us it was hard in the home in Mumbai. All of the boys fought and it was not as nice as it is here. We help him with his laundry and his homework. We are glad we are all together again.

Age Fourteen

I have lived at New Beginnings Children's Home for six years now and am in Standard Seven at school. My time is spent worshipping Jesus, studying in school, doing chores, playing, dancing, and writing. Because I hope to be a dancer when I grow up, I take classical dance lessons. A couple of years ago I started writing. I write letters to Aaie. Sometimes I write poems. I look at my Aaie's photo that I have every day. I still miss her. When I am sad and missing her I pray to Jesus for help. The nightmares have stopped and I have been sleeping well. Jesus has helped me find peace. I like writing poems to remember Aaie – poems like this one:

I was looking for her in every corner
I am still looking but I cannot see her
She raised me in her own body for nine months
She sacrificed a lot and gave me birth
It is a great blessing on my life that she has given birth to me
Even if she was troubled and tortured by my Baba
She went through life and suffered without saying a word
I love my Aaie, she was great for her boys and girls
She was able to understand our hearts and minds
She was crying and tears would fall off
Whenever something would hurt us
We would say Aye
She would ask what happened my child
But those who do not have an Aaie, how can they live?
How the rest of the world calls them orphans
Considers them less or no good
Considers them inferior and worst of the poor lower caste
The baby that cries says Aaie, Aaie dies
But whatever happens we still need to remember Aaie
You cannot forget her no matter how old you grow
Do not ever forget

Trisha getting ready to perform at her school dance

Kishan praying during morning worship

About meeting Trisha

The children of this family were wonderful to meet and spend time with at the home. Trisha has an infectious energy. She loves to play, especially pillow fights. She was always trying to get us to eat one of her delicious mud pies that she and Leena would make while playing in the yard. Her younger brother Kishan was very shy, but could always be found playing cricket or board games. All of these children had beautiful smiles in this family and Kishan has captured my heart on many occasions. Shreya was definitely the surrogate mother of this small family. She looked out for all of her younger sisters and brother. She was quick to make sure they were behaving well and doing their homework and chores. Shreya insisted that she did not remember her mother when we interviewed her. Which was surprising because Trisha remembered everything explicitly. She also told us Shreya was there with her when her mother was killed. Shreya told us it was an accident and that she could not really remember her at all. But one afternoon Shreya and her best friend were teaching me how to wash my clothes. We asked her who taught all of this to her? Shreya answered very quickly, "My Aaie."

Statistics on women being burned to death are staggering in India. Per India's National Crime Records Bureau (http://ncrb.gov.in/adsi2013/adsi2013.htm), one woman every hour is killed in India. They are killed if their family can't meet the groom or his family's dowry demands for not producing male children, or just because they are women. When we were preparing to come to India we read several books to prepare for the culture. One of the books talked about woman being burned to death in India. It was hard for us to grasp. We thought this author was exaggerating and then we heard a first-hand account from a beautiful young woman who suffered for years with nightmares from witnessing this murder. There was no justice for Trisha's mother. This was not the only family of children we interviewed where the mother had been burned to death. But, it was the only one where the children witnessed the murder and could say it was no accident. Many of these incidents go down as accidents. We imagine if we added all the accidental burnings to the national Crime Records Bureau report, the numbers would be much higher than one an hour.

Trisha's father is now visiting the children once a year since Kishan moved to the home. Trisha and Shreya both think he is now a Christian. Trisha hopes that he has been forgiven.

Trisha in the middle of a pillow fight

Rani showing us her bed

Trisha and friend at New Beginnings Children's Home

Rani playing house

Trisha's picture of the garden at New Beginnings Children's Home

Trisha and Rani ready for a school dance performance with two friends

Arun

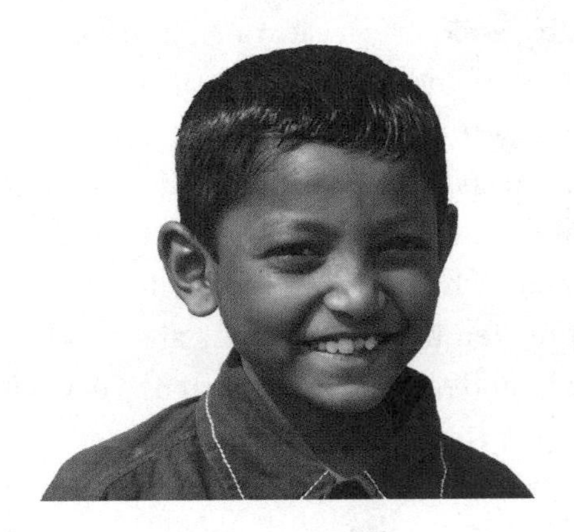

Age Seven

I am Arun. I live with my two-year-old brother Sanjiv, Aaie, Baba, Nani, and Nana. We have much trouble in our home. Aaie wants to become a Christian. Baba tells me that we are Hindu and he does not want a Christian wife. Aaie talks to Baba and his parents about the love of Jesus, and how He can help us. Nani yells and hits Aaie saying she is forbidden to be a Christian. They are always fighting in our home now that Aaie wants to be a Christian. The pastor came and talked with our family. Baba says it is all right for Aaie to study the teachings, but it is not right for her to be baptized. She must stop this because it is upsetting his parents.

Aaie and Baba are fighting again. Baba is hitting her over and over again. She tells him that she will take his sons and go live with her parents. Nani now is involved in the fight. She brings Baba a board and tells him to kill Aaie. I grab Baba's arm and yell at Aaie to just leave, please leave. Aaie picks up

Sanjiv and leaves. She yells for me to follow and come to her parents' house. Baba and Nani are very upset with me. They are yelling at me for grabbing Baba's arm. When they calm down, Nani tells me that my Aaie is very bad, that I must stay here with Baba, and never visit Aaie. I am scared and tired. I wonder when Aaie and Sanjiv will return.

Baba goes to see Aaie and when he comes back he tells me that Sanjiv will stay with Aaie and that I will stay with him. I am upset and want to visit Aaie. Nani tells me I must never visit Aaie. I know where Aaie lives but I'm afraid to go because it will upset my family then. Nani is always saying how bad Aaie is as a wife and mother. I don't listen to her, but I do worry about Baba.

Baba is sick and I spend my days helping him. He sends me to sell different things from our home to buy food for us. Since Aaie left a few months ago, Baba has gotten worse. He is coughing bad and looks very thin. I do my best to take care of him. I help him all day long until Nani and Nana get back from their work. We can't afford to send him to the doctor.

One day at the market I see Aaie and Sanjiv. I hug Aaie and she says she prays for me every day. I tell her how sick Baba is right now. She said that if Baba got worse I should come right to her and not stay with Nani and Nana. I tell her I will come to her if things get worse with Baba. She hugs me very tight and tells me she loves and misses me very much. I walk back to Baba and wonder if I should tell him that I saw Aaie. I get there and Baba is worse. I decide to not tell him so that I don't upset him. I take care of Baba that day and when Nana and Nani come home they are very concerned for Baba.

Baba is very sick and he calls me over and tells me I should leave and go live with Aaie. He tells me that she will take good care of me and that I must go. He is very sick and it is important that he knows I am with Aaie. I tell him then that I saw Aaie at the market. He tells me to go to her and always remember him. I don't understand why Baba is sending me away. I do what he says and go to Aaie. She is very glad that I am with her.

Age Eight

My Baba has died. Aaie says we cannot go to his funeral, that Nani and Nana do not want us there. I hear Aaie, Nani, and Nana talking about Baba's parents threats. There is concern they will want to hurt Sanjiv and me. I am very afraid and do not understand why they would want to hurt us. Aaie and Nani think maybe we should move to another city. Aaie wants to wait and see if things calm down. It is not our fault that Baba died.

Living with Aaie is very busy. She teaches me the Bible and I see her teaching ladies in our village about the Bible too. Aaie is the happiest I have ever seen her. Her brothers, my uncles, say that Aaie should be careful of spreading this Christian faith. Aaie's family is also Hindu. Both of my uncles worship Hindu gods and they walk away when Aaie is reading or teaching from the Bible. But, her parents don't seem to mind. My Aunty also becomes a Christian from Aaie's teaching her. They do not fight in this house like my old one. Aaie is always reading her Bible to them and sharing what she is learning. She takes me to church with her on Sundays. She works with the pastor on a program to pass out Bibles in our village.

One day the pastor and Aaie sit down to talk with me about going to a school in another town. They say I will live at the home during the school year and come home to be with Aaie during school breaks. This is a chance for me to go to school. I will have food, school clothes, and books at this home. Aaie carefully tells me that it is not safe for me in the village with the threats from Baba's family. I don't understand and don't want to live away from Aaie and Sanjiv. Aaie tells me when Sanjiv is six years old he will come to school with me too. She tells me it is a Christian home where I will learn about Jesus. She says she will come visit me when she can and that I will come home on school breaks to live with her.

Aaie and the pastor take me to the home. When we are there Aaie insists on staying for meals. She and I think the food is excellent. She inspects the room where I will sleep. She visits the school I will attend. She talks for a long time with the house parents while I play with the other boys. I like the home but do not like leaving Aaie. When it comes time for her to leave she tells the house parents, "From now on this is your son, if something happens to me you take care of him, and raise him as your own child."

One day my uncle is at the home asking to visit with me. I don't understand why he is here. He takes me by the hand and says I am to come home with him to visit. I am very confused because this is not a school break and I tell him so. I go for a walk with him and he tells me that Aaie is in the hospital. He tells me it was a horrible accident. Aaie was heating milk for Sanjiv and she turned and knocked over a kerosene lamp. Her saree caught fire and it was too well pinned and it burned her severely because they could not get her saree off of her. They rolled her on the ground but it was too late.

I get to the home where Aaie lived with her parents and Nana tells me he rolled Aaie and took her straight to the hospital in a rickshaw. He said she is burned very badly and that we will visit her later. I pray to Jesus to help her. Aunty comes in very upset about Aaie. She too sits and prays with me for Aaie. When we get to the hospital Aaie is in a ward with other patients that have burns. Everyone in the room is a woman. Aaie is covered with bandages and tubes. She can barely talk. I hear her make Nana promise her that Sanjiv and I will be sent to the Christian school to be raised as Christians. Nana promises her that we will go to the Christian school. Soon after, Aaie dies.

Arun and friends at New Beginnings Children's Home

Arun showing us a letter and picture of his sponsors

She is gone. Sanjiv is three and I am eight. We are now orphans. Aunty is very upset. We talk about how Aaie is with Jesus now. We try to find comfort in that she is now with Jesus and in no more pain. Aunty talks with my uncle about a Christian burial for Aaie. Aaie's family says that will not happen, that she will be buried in the proper Hindu way. Now there is fighting in this house. Aunty is insisting that Aaie be buried as a Christian. I also get involved telling my uncles that Aaie would not want a Hindu burial because she is a Christian. She would want a Christian service and burial. The pastor stops by and he also encourages Nani, Nana, and my uncles that Aaie would have wanted a Christian service. The answer was a firm "No!" from my uncles.

The next day we went to Aaie's funeral. Her funeral was at the riverbank and there was a large funeral pyre. Aaie was covered with a white cloth and there were flowers. There was chanting and Aunty was crying and upsetting the family. One of my uncles took Aunty and tied her to a chair. He told her to be quiet, and that she was disturbing the funeral rites. I told my other uncle this is not what my Aaie wanted. He put his hands firmly on my shoulders told me to be quiet, turned me around, and made me watch. My other uncle left my Aunty crying and tied to the chair, then went to light the funeral pyre. It was a long fire and I prayed for my Aunty who was very upset. When the fire was done, we all went home and were made to bathe. Two days later my uncles went to get Aaie's ashes and took them to put in the Ganga River. We stayed in the house mourning Aaie for ten days, as is Hindu tradition.

After ten days were up, Nana asked me if I wanted to go back to the home. I told him yes, and he said he would honor my Aaie's wish for me to go to this home for school. We discussed that Sanjiv would join me when he turned six. At school break, I would return to Nana and Nani's home to be with Sanjiv. I was taken back to school by my uncle. He and I talked a great deal on the train ride back to the home. He tells me that he thinks that Jesus was a teacher and that it is fine to understand His teachings. But, there are many gods and we should embrace them all. I tell him that Jesus is the Lord and Savior. I tell him that I believe as did my Aaie. He does not agree.

Age Ten

It has been almost two years since Aaie died and I think of her often. I am going to be a pastor when I grow up because I want to be just like my Aaie, and teach other people about Jesus and how he saves us. Jesus is now my Baba, Aaie, Nana, and Nani. Jesus is my everything. Whenever I pray to Him, He gives His hand in my hand and protects me from all evil. In school, I study hard to make good grades. At the home, I study the Bible and memorize scripture. I can recite all of Psalm 23 from memory. The most important thing to me is to grow up to be a pastor.

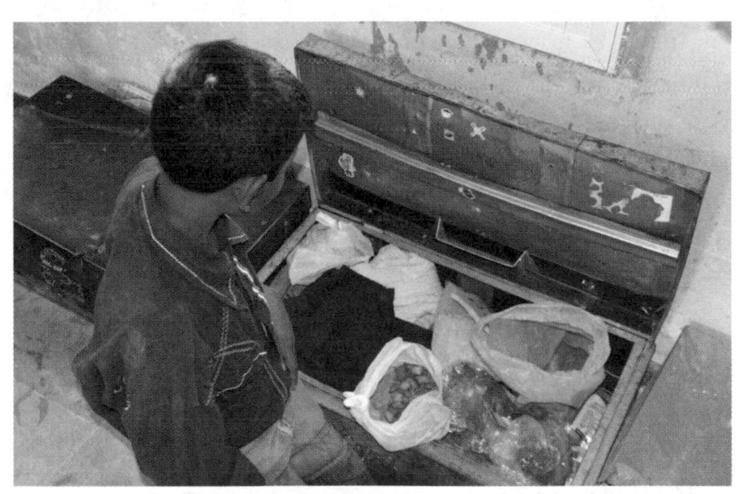

Arun sharing the contents in his trunk. He likes to save food

Arun doing chores

I see Sanjiv on breaks from school. He will join me here at the home next year when he is six I tell him how nice it is here. When I'm on break I'm not allowed to attend church. Nana and Nani tell Sanjiv that he is not allowed to go to church either, but they will honor their promise to Aaie for him to attend school at the Christian home. Otherwise, they want me to be a Hindu. I just pray on my own when I am on break. I also pray for Nana, Nani, and my uncles to come to know Jesus. Sanjiv and I like to play cricket. I tell him we will play cricket many times when he comes to live with me at the home. I will also look out for him, and most importantly, teach him about Jesus.

The Lord is my shepherd; I shall not want.
He makes me lie down in green pastures,
He leads me beside quiet waters,
He refreshes my soul.
He guides me along the right paths for his name's sake.
Even though I walk through the darkest valley,
I will fear no evil, for you are with me;

Your rod and your staff they comfort me.
You prepare a table before me in the presence of my enemies.
You anoint my head with oil; my cup overflows.
Surely your goodness and love will follow me all the days of my life, and I will dwell in the house of the Lord forever. (Psalm 23 NIV)

About meeting Arun

Arun is the most remarkable ten-year-old we have ever met. He is smaller than the other boys his age but he makes up for it with an intensity and drive that is amazing. He can always be found engaged with the other boys in the home. In disputes, you can be sure Arun will stop the fight and have everyone stop and pray about the situation. One time we found him praying in a corner about a disagreement he had with another boy. He wanted to get Jesus involved to help them. He enjoys playing cricket and studying History in school. In Sunday School, with the children, we decided to reenact the anointing of King David. We immediately knew who our King David would be – little Arun, who is slight in size but has a heart for God just like King David.

It is hard to describe an unreached nation until we learned from being in one. It is very different to see shrines built around rocks, and dolls, and images. In one town we visited, they worshiped a large orange rock. There were flowers and gifts laid at the rock. A shrine was built around the rock. Incense was constantly burning in the shrine. We would see women every day dressed in the same color of orange going to pray at the rock. One of the women we met worshiped this rock. I asked her why she worshiped the rock and she did not answer, but just smiled. I really did want to try to understand what she thought the rock would do for her. We saw elaborate shrines with dolls that represent different Hindu gods where people would always be praying and offering flowers or gifts. Each of the pastors we worked with in India told us the need for pastors was great. That it is a hard life for Christian pastors in India. Christians are considered lower than the lowest caste, and pastors face martyrdom.

Arun's picture of the mountains around the children's home

Sitting on the wall taking a break from playing

Arun will be one of these brave pastors, as was his mother. He constantly recited scripture to us, and when he shared about his life, his hands were very demonstrative. We felt like he was preaching to us on several occasions. His eyes were full of courage and hope, and we cannot even imagine the impact this young man will have on the kingdom when he comes of age. He will be a dynamic, engaging, and charismatic preacher of the Word. Arun takes God's word very seriously and pays very close attention in the daily Bible study, and in church on Sunday. He memorizes full verses of Scripture, and his favorite is Psalm 23. We believe that God has a firm hand on this young man's life and he is going to be mightily used in this 98 percent unreached nation.

Arun sharing his story with us

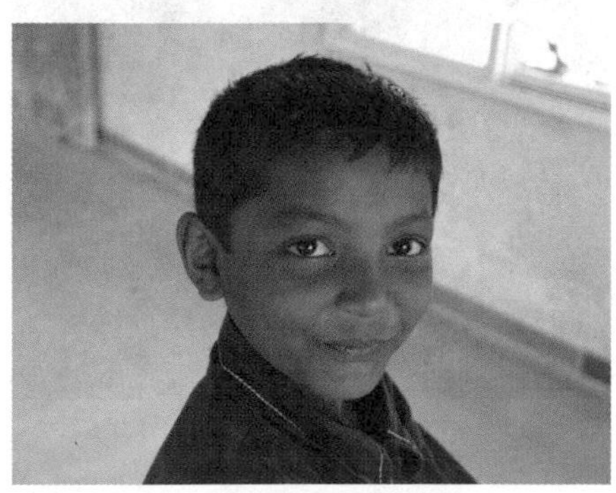

Arun posing for a photo

Arun playing cricket

Praying during morning devotions

Nilesh

Age Eighteen

I am Nilesh, named after the Hindu god Krishna. Aaie is Hindu and follows all of the Hindu rituals. She worships the goddess Lakshmi, the goddess of abundance. In our home there is a whole shrine for the goddess Lakshmi. Aaie can be found praying to Lakshmi for help with all her troubles. She gives Lakshmi flowers and food. Our house smells of the incense Aaie burns to please the goddess. I ask Aaie if the goddess answers her when she asks the goddess for help. Aaie believes the goddess looks out for our family and that we need to believe in her and the abundance she gives our family.

I do not believe in the Hindu gods, goddesses, or gurus. I believe in Jesus. Jesus is the living God. The gurus are just human beings, and the Hindu gods and goddesses are made up. I have studied Jesus and the Bible for the last eleven years. I attend a Christian church and want to be baptized. At this time, I cannot be baptized because Aaie does not support my decision. I hope to attend Bible College after I pass my Standard Ten exams. I think maybe I will be baptized when I am at Bible College. It is a tough decision to make because if I am baptized, Aaie will disown me, and never speak with me again. She will not help me to arrange a marriage and I could even lose my job. I want to be a pastor and I pray for God to open her eyes and soften her heart.

I lived for ten years, from the age of seven to seventeen, in New Beginnings Children's Home. This is where I learned about my Savior, Jesus Christ. I came to live at New Beginnings Children's Home a year after my Baba died in a motorcycle accident. This accident changed our lives forever. Our family was a higher cast, Viashya, and Baba had a good job at the spice factory. Aaie stayed home and raised my older brother, Prem, and me. When Baba died, Aaie was very scared. I remember her crying. We were fortunate because Aaie and Prem were able to get jobs at the spice factory. They both worked eight to twelve hours a day in the factory. This allowed Aaie to keep our home and have food. I was left to myself during the day. I found other kids to hang out with and occasionally got in trouble.

Aaie found out about a home that would take me during the school year and send me home at breaks to live with her and Prem. Since I had lost a parent, the home would help get my education sponsored. She decided this was best for me and sent me to New Beginnings Children's Home. At first, I was very scared at the home. There were a lot of boys and girls living here. The rules were strange to me. I was used to running free all day while Aaie and Prem worked. Here I had to get up at a certain time, do calisthenics, put away my bedroll, shower, do chores, go to daily devotions, eat with other boys, and then go to school. At school I had more rules to follow. It was rough for me the first couple of months. I really missed Aaie and Prem, and my freedom.

Once I made friends and got used to the rules, I loved living at New Beginnings Children's Home. I enjoyed breaks back home with Aaie, too. I shared with her what I was learning about Jesus and at school. She always instructed me that Jesus was just one of many gods, and that I must never leave my Hindu beliefs. She preferred to discuss what I was doing in school instead of church. I always tried to share the Bible with her and the stories and songs I was learning. My favorite song is *One Day I Will Go Afar and See Jesus.*

When I was ten years old, Prem ran away from our home. We have never seen or heard from him again. I wonder what happened to him. Aaie said he did not like working at the spice factory. She was upset to lose him. She said she looks for him when she goes to town. Aaie prays to the goddess Lakshmi for Prem's return. I pray for God to keep Prem safe and for him to return home. Every break I go home and Prem is not back. I rest assured that God knows where Prem is and that He is looking out for him.

Over the years, I even grew to be a leader of the boys at the home. I made sure they got up and led their daily exercises. I was also responsible to check on their chores and make sure the rules were being followed. I would organize cricket and other games to play with the boys during our free time. Occasionally, I helped some of the younger boys with their school work. The boys respected me and followed my direction. One boy who came to the home, Deepak, followed me everywhere. When I graduated Standard Ten and had to leave the home, Deepak took my place as the leader of the boy's room. He and I are still good friends, and I visit him often.

School was not easy for me and I studied hard for my Standard Ten exams. Unfortunately, I did not pass my exams. This meant I could not go directly to college or university. I went home and Aaie got me a job packing spices at the spice factory. I now work eight to ten hours a day, six days a week. I do not like my job. I make $4.00 a day working in the spice factory and then I study hard in the evenings so that when I can retake my exams, I will pass. I sometimes visit New Beginnings Children's Home on Sunday's after church. I like to see Deepak and see how the other boys are doing. We usually play cricket and Frisbee when I visit. I am using this time at home with Aaie to talk with her some more about the Bible and Jesus. She tells me to think and study what I want, but that I can never be baptized.

My friend, Vivek, is in the same situation. He and I attend church together at Fellowship Christian Church. Vivek also did not pass his exams. His father wants him to forget about Bible College and all this Jesus nonsense and keep working at the factory making car clutches. Vivek also makes $4.00 a day but he only works eight hours a day, six days a week. He also shares with his parents about Jesus and what he learns at church. Vivek's family is Buddhist, but they seem just as against Vivek being a Christian as my Hindu family is against me being a baptized Christian.

Vivek and I talk about why we want to be pastors. Vivek wants to be a pastor to help him stay and live in the presence of God. I want to be a pastor to serve God and share the good news with other people. Both of us will be disowned by our families when we are baptized. This will make it hard for us to find wives, jobs, and support. We will be completely dependent on our church and God. We both trust God will take care of us and see us through when we are baptized.

About meeting Nilesh

It was an honor to meet both Nilesh and Vivek when we attended services at Fellowship Christian Church. Both young men also visited with us at New Beginnings Children's Home. They are very energetic and on fire for Jesus. Both of them are willing to face the hardships of losing their families to follow Jesus. For Nilesh, this also means leaving one of the higher castes and the benefits that provides for him. As a pastor, he will be below the Untouchables caste in his society's view. He does not seem to be worried about this, although he shared his fervent prayer is for his mother to accept his being a Christian.

Nilesh and Deepak

Nilesh playing cricket with the boys

We could see as he hung out with the other children at New Beginnings Children's Home how much the other boys respected and listened to him. Even Deepak followed him around the entire time he was sharing with us in his interviews. It was nice to see Nilesh have fun with the other boys. He played both cricket and Frisbee until he had to head back home for the night.

Both Nilesh and Vivek give most of the money they make to support their families. Vivek is helping his father pay back a loan he took out. Vivek shared that he fights constantly with his father about going to college when he passes his exams. His father wants him to work and help the family. Vivek thinks his mother will ultimately accept him as a Christian, but that his father never will. In Nilesh's situation, his money is used to help support himself and his mother.

Nilesh quickly referenced Bible verses in our discussion with him and has a genuine desire to serve God. He wants to lead his mother to Jesus and then lead other people throughout India to Jesus as well. His college or seminary school is already supported by his New Beginnings Children's Home sponsor. He just has to pass his exams. When we asked him what we could pray for him, he asked that we pray for his mother to change her heart and mind for Jesus. He shared that if his mother does not change her mind by the time he is in seminary, then he will go ahead and be baptized while he is there. He does pray for his mother to change her mind. The church assured us that if either of these young men lose their families' support they will help them to arrange a marriage and support them in their ministry.

Nilesh assisting the boys set up a game

Nilesh's picture of the mountains

Nilesh playing outside with the boys

Nilesh and one of the younger boys

Pari

Age Five

I am waiting with my older sisters, Riya and Radha, to see what the new baby Aaie is having will be. Will it be a boy or girl baby? Baba and Aaie both discuss this baby being a boy. Radha is the oldest, age nine, and she says if this baby is a boy then there will be no more babies. Riya, age seven, is excited that there will be a new baby for her to play with. I will now be a big sister too. Baba comes out and he does not look happy. We go in our hut and Aaie has the baby. She is also very sad. Nani is holding the new baby and she looks angry. We have a new baby sister. Avani is her name. I ask Radha why Baba and Aaie are both sad. She tells me it is because another girl baby has come.

We live on a cotton farm in a hut. Aaie and Baba are cotton pickers. Nana, Radha, and Riya help in the fields. They work in the fields from early morning until it starts to get dark. It is hard work and they get cuts from the cotton plant when they pull out the cotton. Someday when I am big enough to carry a bag I will pick cotton too. For now, I get to stay at our hut and help Nani take care of my new baby sister. I also help clean the dishes and with the cooking. It is better when there is cotton in the fields for us to pick because when there is cotton we have money for food. We move from field to field to pick the cotton as it is ready. When it is the rainy season and when there is no cotton to pick, Baba, Nana, and Aaie work some in the fields, and any other work they can get. Baba sometimes works fixing tires.

Age Seven

Aaie is with child again. We are all asking the gods to bring a boy baby this time. I remember how sad and angry everyone was when Avani was born. I love Avani. She is two now and I enjoy helping to take care of her, and playing with her. She likes me to chase her and she thinks she plays kho kho with me. Aaie is very quiet about this baby but she told my oldest sister, Radha, that the gods must bless us with a boy this time. A brother would be nice, but I like little sisters.

I am old enough to work in the fields picking cotton now. I miss Avani and Nani. It was easier to work at the hut than it is in the cotton fields. I carry a bag that hangs at my side. I work to pick the cotton and get as much into my hands as I can then stuff it into the bag. As I work, I get many sharp cuts on my hands and arms. They leave marks on me as they heal. I have gotten better at picking the cotton, and don't get cut by the bristles around the cotton as much as I did when I started. The bag gets heavier as I pick and once it is full I walk to the end of the row and put it on our family's sheet.

The days in the cotton field are long and hard and hot. My sisters and I talk as we work up and down the rows all day long. It is hard for Aaie to pick because she is large with the baby who is due to be born any day now. She does not pick as much as usual. We take one break for food. When we leave our cotton at our family's sheet there is water we can drink. Baba gets paid for what we all pick. I don't know how much he gets paid. My sisters and I don't get paid for our work. All the money goes to Baba to help our family.

Our family is very happy the new baby came and he is a boy. Everyone is happy and celebrating the birth of our baby brother, Aditiya. He was born during the night. Baba and Aaie are placing thanks offerings to the gods for blessing us with a son. Nani and Nana are very excited too and share the news with our village. There is no crying like there was when Avani was born. Great joy!

Age Nine

Aditiya is growing big. He is two years old and brings Baba and Aaie great joy. I notice that when we are low on food that Aditiya gets a full plate of food even if we girls have less to eat. This is upsetting to me because I work hard in the fields and get hungry. Radha and Riya say we are not to speak about this. Radha is to be married. She does not seem happy with this news. Girls in our village are married from the age of thirteen and older. Radha is now turning thirteen. She does not know the man she will be married to and will meet him on her wedding day.

Nana and Nani tell her it is a good thing to be married. She will leave us when she is married and live in another village with her husband's family. She will be expected to help her husband's mother and take good care of her. Radha works hard in the fields and I think she will not have any trouble working hard for her new husband's family. I will miss her as she is very quick to help us younger sisters and to explain things to us.

There has been a pastor visiting our village and he talked to Baba about taking Riya and me to school. He tells Baba about a children's home that will send us to school, clothe, and feed us.

They discuss that when Avani is old enough in two years, she can come to school too. We would live at the school and then come home on breaks. I don't know about going to school. In our village only some of the boys go to school. They wear uniforms and walk two miles to the school building. It is expensive to go to school and not too many of the families can afford to send their children to school. It is viewed in our village that education, if it can be afforded, should be for the boys.

Baba and Aaie tell Riya and me that they have decided to send us to school. Aaie is excited that her daughters will have an education to read and write. She tells us that there will be sponsors who pay for our food, clothes, books, medical care, and education. I don't want to leave my family and am very scared at the idea of going off to another city to go to school. Aaie says they will not be able to afford to visit us, but that they will see us back at home every school break. Baba says we will go to school until he arranges for our marriages.

We leave for New Beginnings with the pastor. It is a long train ride to the city where the school is located. I had never been on a train before, and it was exciting to travel by train. When Riya and I get to New Beginnings it was different from living in our hut. We are given beds to sleep in and new clothes to wear. We have to see a doctor and have an exam to make sure we are healthy. There is plenty of food here and girls get the same amount of food as boys. At first, the rules were very hard for me to follow, but I got used to them very quickly.

Riya loves it here and she has made friends with many of the girls. I have made a few friends too. We are both in the class together in school, which is very nice. We help each other study so we can work to catch up with our friends in the older classes. We are learning about Jesus at New Beginnings. Every morning we sing songs and hear teachings from the Bible. Riya and I had never heard of Jesus before coming here.

Pari and Avani

Pari doing calisthenics

Age Thirteen

I am finishing Standard Four at the government school the children at New Beginnings Children's Home attend. Riya, Avani, and I will be going home for break in a couple of weeks. We all talk about missing the food when we go home. It will be good to see Nani, Nana, Baba, Aaie, and Aditiya. Aditiya does not go to school at New Beginnings. Baba pays for him to go to the school near our home. Baba says Aditiya must go to a school close to home. I also notice that Aditiya does not work in the cotton fields like Radha, Riya, Avani, and me did. Baba and Aaie take very special care of Aditiya.

Riya is nervous about going home this time. Last break Baba said he was concerned she was getting old and that he should be arranging her marriage. Riya told him and Aaie that she would like to finish school and go to college. Baba says a girl should be married by the time she is sixteen. She is fifteen this year. Riya does not want to be married. She told me that she would like to finish school and become a doctor.

We take the train back to our village and I am shocked at how big Aditiya has gotten this year. He is now six years old and has finished Standard One in school. He likes to play cricket with the other school boys he has as friends. He is lucky that he does not have to work in the cotton fields and that Baba will pay for him to go to school. Riya, Avani, and I are blessed because we are learning about Jesus and He has given us sponsors for our care and schooling. We share with our family what we learn about Jesus. Aaie tells us the pastor comes and shares with them about Jesus too.

I hear Riya arguing with Baba. We are not supposed to argue with him. She is telling him no, that she will not be married, that she wants to finish school. He is telling her that she will do what she is told to do. He will decide when she will be married, and he says that she should have been married by now. He tells her that she does not need more education as a woman. They keep arguing and Baba grabs her and takes her outside. He yells for me and Avani to come too.

Baba drags Riya over to the Babool tree. He ties her hands and legs to the tree. Aaie gives a look that we know means we are to stay quiet. I see the long, sharp thorns on the tree are cutting Riya where she is tied to the tree. Baba cuts a switch off the tree and starts to beat her. Riya cries and begs for him to stop. Each hit makes her flinch and move. Her moving makes the thorns cut deeper and she bleeds. She yells out, "I will marry, I will marry," and she is crying! I am so scared and Avani is squeezing my hand very hard. Baba finally stops beating Riya. He looks at Avani and me. We both stand perfectly still. He says this is what happens to daughters that don't obey their fathers. Then he leaves us. Aaie tells us to go back to our hut and she comes with us leaving Riya tied to the bush, crying. Baba finally comes and unties Riya after two hours.

Babool Tree

Pari playing carrom

It is not a good school break. Riya, Avani, and I barely speak. We do what we are told and wait for the time to go back to school. The Pastor visits us and has a long talk with Baba. Baba tells the pastor that Riya will not be returning to school, that she is needed to help care for her brother and work the fields. We know the truth is she will be married while we are at school and move to another village. Just like Radha, we will rarely see her, if ever again. Avani and I return to school after break.

About meeting Pari

Pari is a beautiful, intelligent thirteen-year-old girl. She loves to hear stories from the Bible and declares them all to be her favorite. As we talked with Pari about her life, she was clearly upset that her sister, Riya, did not return to school. The mission's team suspected that the plan was for Riya to be married. The family told them that Riya was needed to care for her younger brother. Once Pari told her whole story, there was great concern for not only Riya, but also for Avani's and Pari's future. The mission told us the pastors would go and speak again with

Pari's father, but since these children had parents, they did not have a way to force them to let the girls finish school.

Pari enjoyed her time working with us. She was getting ready for a school dance performance and performed it for us to see. She is a beautiful dancer. We saw her playing a dance game the girls liked, called, "Hey Girl." This is a dance/song the girls learned in school, in their English class. The girls would stand in a circle with one in the middle who would dance around and stop in front of a girl. This girl would switch places with the original girl, and the game would go on. The girls sing,

> "Little Sally Walker, walking down the street.
> She didn't know what to do so she stopped in front of me.
> She said, 'Hey girl, do your thing, do your thing and switch!
> Hey girl, do your thing, do your thing and switch!'"

Pari playing "Hey Girl"

Pari would jump up and down with excitement as the dancer went around the circle looking for the next dancer to choose. Her excitement was infectious and we joined in the dance too.

Pari picks me to dance with her

We noticed that Pari was a hard worker and could be found getting her chores done and helping in the kitchen when she was not playing. Her favorite food is bananas or apples. She also likes to learn English in school. She practiced talking with us during her interview and free time. She also looks out for her younger sister. When we talked with Avani, she shared that Pari helps her with her schoolwork and with doing her hair. Avani is a very strong-willed little girl and we found that Avani was in almost every picture we took at the children's home. She was quick to jump in the picture when we had the camera out. She was constantly asking us to take a photo and then show it to her. Pari would smile sweetly and try to help us get pictures of kids without Avani in every one. She thought she should be in every picture we took. One time we asked her to wait while we took another child's photo and she snuck around and stuck her head in the picture.

Pari wants to be a nurse and help people when she grows up. She discussed her plans to finish school at New Beginnings and then go to University to study in a nursing program. I asked her if she thought this would happen. She got very quiet and said, "Not if my Baba has me get married. Then I will be a wife and pick cotton for life. My life would be over." I asked her what she wanted me to share about her, and she said, "Tell them how difficult my life is as a cotton picker from a small farm hut, that it hurts when Baba drinks, and, to pray for my sister, Riya, to heal from her beating and to have a good marriage, and maybe a husband who will let her go to school."

Pari's picture of her home at New Beginnings Children's Home

Pari during morning worship

Pari doing laundry

Avani taking care of the goat

Raju

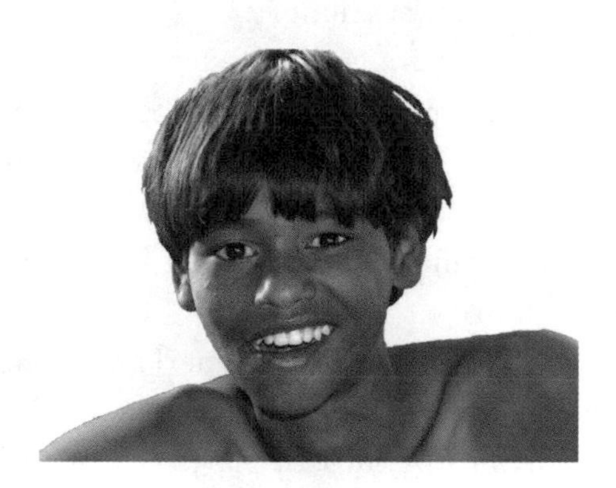

Age Eight

Today is another day on the train. Aaie will carry my one-year-old brother, Nitin, with her. Baba will sit at the train station begging for money while the three of us ride the trains. Baba has trouble walking and it is best for him to beg in front of the station. Aaie helps him walk to and from the station every day. Aaie will carry Nitin with her for most of the day as she walks through the trains begging. Aaie will ride the trains going north, and I will work the trains going south. This way we don't each ask the same passengers for money. We make more this way. I used to ride with Aaie all day, but now I am big enough to help get money for our family. I do miss staying with her all day because she helped protect me from angry passengers that hit or kick me. I work cleaning the train for money. Baba taught me to take off my shirt and clear the floors of trash. I take my shirt and push all the trash and dirt out of each train compartment. I then push it out of the train. When I finish each compartment, I hold out my hand hoping someone will pay me for clearing out the trash. I repeat this through the whole train. Today it is a good ride because I have made twenty rupees and find some discarded food to eat on the train floor. I am always hungry.

As I grow bigger, I am getting faster and stronger. When passengers try to hit or kick me, I'm able to move quickly so it does not hurt as much as it used to when I was younger. As I get bigger it is also easier to jump from the trains. I think it's fun to leap off the train as it passes where I get off to switch to a northbound train.

When I'm waiting for a train to come, I have friends – other boys who also beg at the stations to help their families. Some of the boys are starting to gamble by playing cards while waiting for their next train. A man watches for us and teaches us to play. I try not to play because it costs five rupees, and I have lost all the money I have made several times. Baba and Aaie get upset if I don't bring money back from a day of work. Some of the older boys drink alcohol or sniff shoe glue. They say it makes them feel better and not hungry. I have not tried the alcohol or shoe glue, but my friends do these things. Today I spent extra time with my friends because I had to wait two hours for the train to come. I finally get on a southbound train and start working in each compartment as we head back to the station where I started my day.

As I work cleaning, I hope to find some dropped popcorn or nuts to eat. Smiling at the passengers, I hold out my hand for money. I finish up the train and have made thirty more rupees. That is fifty rupees today. I then sit at the open door in the middle of the train and let the wind cool me off. I'm dirty from sweeping the compartments of trash and dirt. I put my dirty shirt back on. I wonder how Baba and Aaie did today. I hope Baba did not spend all his money on alcohol. When that happens there is not much money for us to get food.

I won't always work the trains. I think someday I will be a policeman.

Age Ten

Where we live is made of cardboard, plastic, and we have a metal scrap roof. It is not much, but it keeps us dry, and there is a well close to our village where we go to get water for cooking and cleaning. Every day is the same for us. Get up to work, and if we are lucky, have breakfast and chai. Then we walk to the train station to start our day begging. Once our day is done we all head back to our village. On good days we get enough for a small meal, but on bad days we only have chai. Aaie reminds us that we have no relatives, and all we have is each other, so we work together to support our family.

Baba is getting sick and I am afraid for him. He now has to be helped to the train station each day to beg. I have to let him lean on me and I try to hold him up. He curses at me if he falls. I try to be very careful and help him. He is losing weight and some days he's too ill to go begging. Aaie will not bring him alcohol on the days he can't beg. If I have a good day, I try to sneak him some alcohol. This always makes him happy and he calls me a good son.

We had a bad day today. There was not much money made begging and I lost most of mine playing cards. Baba was angry because there was not enough money for him to get any alcohol. Nitin is three years old and he is making it hard for Aaie to work her train. Sometimes she gives him something to make him sleep so she can work the train. She says it will not hurt him, that she did this to me when I was little too. She will put him in a safe place on the train to sleep while she works. He has trouble sleeping at nights when he has slept on the train all day. I think this is bad as we need to sleep to work the trains the next day.

I think about how some of the other boys have started picking pockets. They have showed me how to do this. First, you watch for the biggest wallet by looking at how big the bulge is in the man's pocket. The bigger the bulge, the more money is in the wallet. Some of my friends have stopped begging and spend their time picking pockets. They say that there is more money doing this. I watch some of them do this again and again at the train stations. They take the wallet and quickly head far away from the person they took it from. Once they are clear, they get all the money from the wallet and then throw it away. I know how to do it, but I am afraid of the police. I got caught by the police last year and they beat me for begging. I don't know what they would do to me if they caught me picking pockets. They watch for pickpockets. When I see the police, I run very fast to get away from them. I am a fast runner.

Sometimes, though, I am not fast enough. A new boy started working our train lines and three of us boys decided to beat him up so he would stop. The police saw us hitting him and caught us. I did not see them soon enough to run away. They took us to the jail and beat us. We were there for three days without any food. It was scary to be in jail. Aaie and Baba did not know where I was or what had happened. Aaie finally heard about the fight and that the police had arresting me with two other boys. She was glad when I came home. Baba and Aaie warned me to be careful and stay out of the way of the police. I will be more careful to watch for the police. It is bad for us to lose my work for three days.

Other boys spend their days trying to beat the card games at the stations or playing dice. There are lots of ways to lose money at the train stations. The men who run the games make a lot of money off the train boys. I used to avoid these games, but now I play the games when I can. Since I am bigger and I learned other boys get to keep part of their money, Aaie lets me keep half of what I make begging. I spend this money usually playing these games. My friends and I try to figure out ways to win. Rarely do we win, most of the time we lose our money. It is still fun and a break from our work. We have to watch for the police while we play these games too. They will arrest the men who run the games and the boys who pay to play them.

Picture of a train station in India

There are men that sell us boys drugs. We can get alcohol, rags with whitening fluid, shoe glue, or smack (low grade injectable heroin). Sometimes, I buy shoe glue because it costs little money. I sniff it and it makes me feel brave and not hungry. It takes much of the pain away from my feet that have sores all over them. This time Aaie says it is worms. She gives me something to help. I don't own any shoes and we don't have any money for shoes. Last time I got these sores, I had trouble carrying Baba.

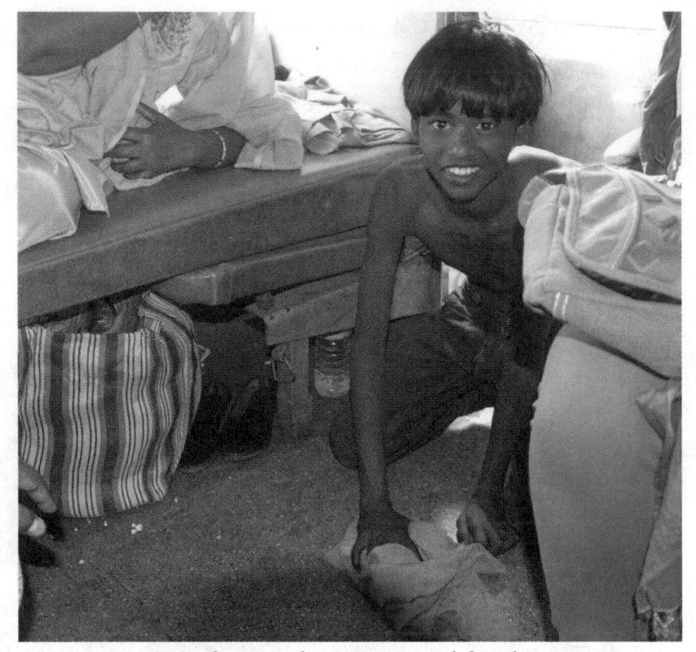

Raju cleaning the train car with his shirt

All of my friends drink alcohol now and some are starting to use smack that leaves long thin scars on their arms. They say when people see the marks or smell the alcohol they won't give them money. I think I will stay with shoe glue to feel better. No one can tell I am using it and I think I can stop any time. If I have too much, I wake up with my heart pounding in my chest and have a headache. It is the only fun I have other than jumping from the trains.

I won't always work the trains. I think someday I will get a job maybe working construction.

Age Twelve

I am carrying Baba on my back to the train station. He cannot walk at all now. Every day he rides to the train station and back to our village clinging to my back. I also have to carry him in and out to relieve himself. I notice he now pees red. I tell Aaie but she does not say anything. As Baba and I walk along, I talk to him. I tell him about my friends and the trouble they get into, and some of their jokes. All of a sudden, I trip and drop him. He starts to yell and curse at me. I feel very bad and try to get him back up. He is finally back on me and I walk very carefully the rest of the way to the train station. I leave him at his spot. I think today, if I make enough money, I will bring him alcohol to make him happy with me again.

As I ride the train I see pictures for the Bollywood movies. I think one day I will try to see one of these movies. The action ones look best. There is a mall where the movie theater is located. I hear that there is a large screen and soft chairs. The pictures show handsome men and beautiful women who star in the movies. I wonder what it would be like to see a movie. I probably will never see a movie because my friends say you have to wear shoes to see a movie. I sing as I work today because I am happy to have found half a bag of popcorn someone dropped all over a compartment floor. I sweep it up and pick it out of the dirt to eat it. I am making money cleaning today and will be able to get Baba some alcohol. I think how he will call me a good son.

I am riding the train north now and have finished this day's work. I hope Aaie has had a good day too, and that Nitin either slept or helped beg. I sit in the doorway and let the wind rush over me as I look at the fields we are passing. It is a nice rest and my stomach feels good from the popcorn I found. I have made sixty rupees today. I will use most of it to get alcohol for Baba. I will just tell Aaie it was a bad day for me and give her the little money that is left. She does not like for me to buy Baba alcohol. It just makes him so happy with me when I get it for him. I know he does not feel well and this seems to help him feel better.

Raju eating popcorn on the train

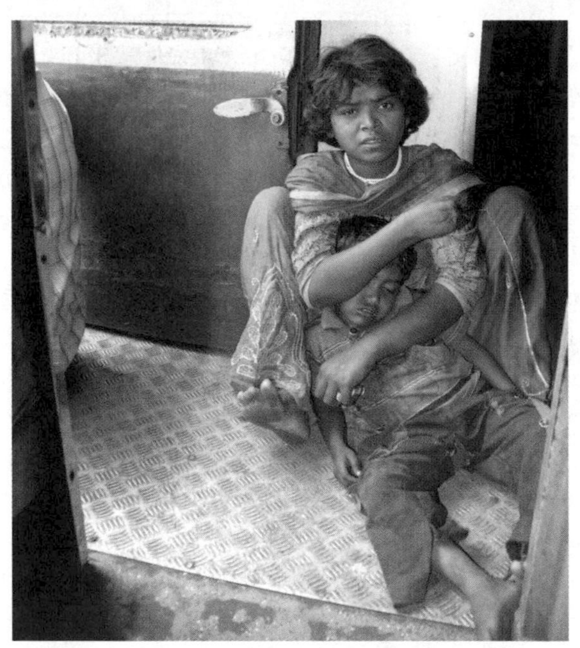

Child that we were told was drugged so he would sleep while his mother begs on the train

I get to the train station and Baba is not in his spot. I think maybe Aaie helped him get home. I pick up his alcohol and hide it in my dirty shirt. I head home and think about Baba's cursing me this morning when I dropped him and how now he will say "good son" to me. I am out of shoe glue, but don't feel too bad. I hope I won't have trouble sleeping. The shoe glue helps me to sleep. My foot is bleeding because one of the sores opened up. I finally get home and Nitin is crying and Aaie is sitting silent. I ask what's wrong and where is Baba. Aaie says Baba died today.

We are Hindu and Baba has a Hindu burial. It is paid for by the government since we have no money. Aaie is very quiet since Baba died. She said I must work hard to help her provide for Nitin. I tell her I will work more trains, jumping the lines to add a few more to my daily coverage. I drink the alcohol I brought for Baba. At first I don't like the taste, but the more I drink, the better I feel. It helps me to not feel hunger or the sores on my feet, and it helps me sleep. I think the alcohol works better than the shoe glue. I remember what my friends say about people on the train not giving money to you if they smell alcohol on you. I decide I will only drink alcohol at night when I am at home. I need to sleep in order to work tomorrow on the trains.

I won't always work the trains. I think someday I will get a job maybe as an actor making a Bollywood movie.

Age Fifteen

Aaie, Nitin, and I all have our own trains we work now. I always smile when one of their trains pass by mine. We never see each other because we are busy working. I have taught Nitin how to clean the compartments with his shirt like I do. He is a hard worker and usually makes fifty rupees a day. Since he is little he gives all his money to Aaie. I still keep half of what I make for myself. When we get home Aaie takes her plate with a picture of the god Hanuman on it and we place our money on the plate. Aaie worships god Hanuman she gives offerings to him and sometimes buys incense to burn for him. She says Hanuman looks out for our family. I think god Hanuman is my favorite god because he is big and strong.

My friends and I use the breaks between train rides to do smack and gamble. This makes the day more fun but I know it is risky. I make sure to only do the smack injections on my right arm which I don't use to reach out when I ask for money. The needles leave lines on my arm, so when I reach out asking for money after cleaning a compartment I always use my left arm so nobody sees any drug lines. I use alcohol to help me sleep at night. I can only do smack when I have a good begging day. My friends are right, it makes me feel good. I think about how to get more. Occasionally, I will pick a pocket to help get money for the smack. I think I can stop anytime I want. It just helps me to feel better.

Statue of Hanuman

I won't always work the trains. I think someday I will get a job maybe as a farmer. I know someday, somehow, I will get off the trains.

About meeting Raju

We went to the train station that day hoping to interview children working or begging on the trains for a living. The train going south we wanted to ride was late. We saw a man with a group of boys around him across the tracks. John, one of the Life Light missionaries with us, said for us to wait and he would go see if he could get any of the boys to talk with us. We were able to take pictures of the boys from across the tracks. They were giving the man money to play a card game with him. This was one of the many men (gamblers, drug dealers, etc.) that use these children to get their money. As the pastor walked over, the group of boys ran away, but the man stayed and talked with him. John returned and told us that the boys had been gambling and ran because they thought he was the police coming toward them. Later on, when we reviewed our photos, we were surprised to see Raju was among the group of boys. In one photo it appears he is doing smack.

Our train finally arrived. It was an interesting train that God placed us on that day. It was overcrowded and full of Sikh pilgrims heading to a pilgrimage site to worship. Some were very cordial and offered to share their compartment with us. We sat down and patiently waited for the train to start moving. It was a hot steamy day and the heat seemed to intensify the smells in the train from all the people tightly packed in, and from the restroom compartments. We were hopeful that the movement of the train would cause a breeze to carry the stifling air away. While we were waiting to leave, one of the Life Light pastors walked up with a train boy for us to talk with. The boy smiled sweetly and began to talk to us as we asked him about his work on the trains. He said his name was Raju and he could talk briefly, but he must get to work. We noticed how thin he was and asked if we could buy him something to eat from the vendors selling snacks on the train. John translated our question and Raju quickly said yes. We got him popcorn and he ate the bag so fast we were concerned he would choke. We followed that with a cup of ice cream that he ate in four quick gulps, earning him his first ice cream headache. He then told us that he had never had an ice cream before and said he liked it very much.

At this point, the Sikh men sharing their compartment with us came back from the train's restroom. They insisted that Raju get out of the compartment. They seemed quite upset that we were talking with this boy. Raju moved to an adjacent seat and we continued to ask Raju about his work on the train. He was eager to show us what he does. We saw the color of his shirt and asked John if he was one of the boys who was gambling. John said maybe, and asked Raju. He answered affirmatively and told John he thought he was the police, so he took off. Raju showed us how he cleans the compartment and then held out his hand to the Sikh men for money. They pointedly ignored him. Raju just smiled and told us he would be back after he cleaned the train.

Once he was gone, the Sikh men wanted John to tell us we should not give any money to that boy, that he will just use it to buy drugs. John assured them we would only provide the boy with food. The men then talked about their pilgrimage and asked questions about us. They seemed pleased to have Americans sharing their compartment. Riding a train in India is an experience itself. The toilet is a hole in the floor of the train over which you squat to use the restroom. As we passed the two restroom compartments, we were relieved we were not seated close to them and we were determined to not use the bathroom, if at all possible for the duration of the trip.

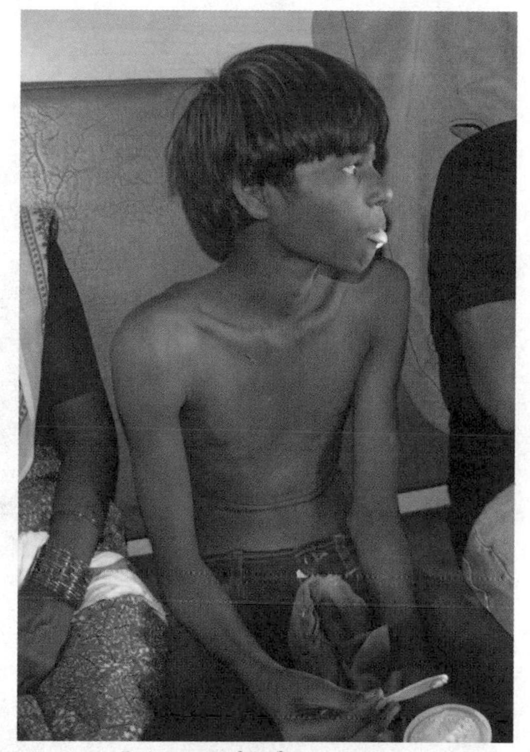

Raju eating his first ice cream

Sikh men that shared our compartment on the train

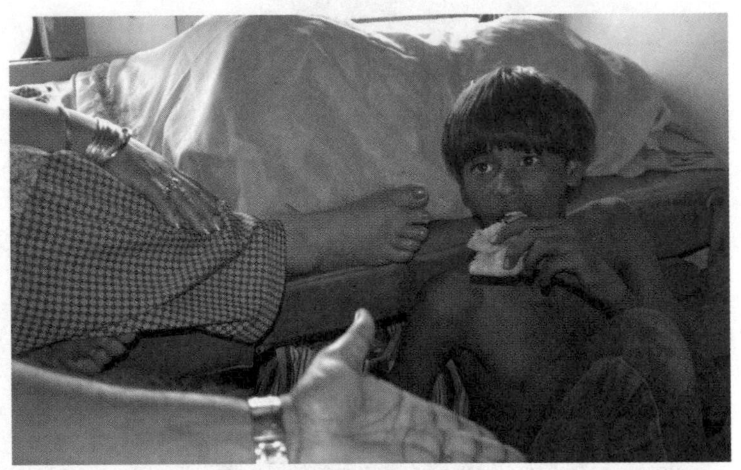

Raju eating chapatti shared with him by the Sikh pilgrims

Raju doing what appears could be smack. The boy is doing something to his right arm.

Soon Raju returned to us beaming and showed us the thirty rupees he made cleaning the train. When we asked what he would do with the money he quickly shared that half would go to his mom. It was hard to talk with him because the train was full of people on this pilgrimage and they all wanted to get involved in our conversation with Raju. For his part, Raju would just shrug, smile, and move wherever he was asked to go and continue to try and talk with us. The Sikhs on the train were serving free meals to the pilgrims. When the food was delivered, the men in our compartment invited us to also join them in eating. We politely declined but inquired if Raju could please have a plate. They would not give him a plate of food, but they were kind enough to give him some bread. One of the men offered me a peanut snack. I took it, thanked him, and told him I would save it for our return trip as we were at our destination.

We departed the train and invited Raju to join us. Our driver knew where we would be getting off the train and was waiting for us there. We continued our conversation with Raju and asked if he would like a ride back home. His face lit up with excitement. When we opened the car door, he jumped in the car and bounced on the seat. He looked around the entire car taking everything in. We learned that this was his very first car ride. He was amazed at how quiet the car was compared to the noisy train. During our car ride, we heard many stories about Raju's life and about his drug use. He showed us the scars on his one arm and kept telling us that he thought he could stop any time he wanted. He shared his best memory of his dad, which was of him yelling and cursing him when he dropped him. This was what he thought about when he remembered his dad.

To thank him for his help we asked if we could take him shopping for clothes, shoes, and some food for his family. He had never owned a pair of shoes and had sores on his feet. Bruce,

John, and the pastors took Raju shopping. He got a solid pair of shoes, underwear, a shirt, and blue jeans. He was selective in looking over the clothes, but not picky. Then, in the grocery store, he did not know what he was supposed to do. John asked if he could help him pick out food. Raju quickly accepted and they picked up beans, flour, cooking oil, and other staples to help the family. We then took Raju back to the mission where he shared with us he never in his life imagined a day like this would happen to him. As he shared about his god Hanuman we shared about our Jesus. He told us he saw a picture once of our Jesus on a cross. We let him get a shower and put on his new clothes. We gave him one final item, a New Testament to take home with him.

John and the pastors asked him if he would like to go to school. Raju said he would but his mom would not allow it since they needed his money to survive. The pastors suggested they could get him a day job on the buses and he could go to night school. Raju thought it would be all right if his mom agreed. We took pictures with Raju and then prayed over him. One of the pastors took Raju and his new things home to meet his mom.

At this time, the pastors have shared with us that they do monthly visits with Raju. His mom has refused to let him get a job on the bus line and to go to night school. Life Light is working to develop a program to help the children that work on the trains.

Raju had great hopes of getting off the train. He insisted at various parts in his story that he would get off the train and become something else. When he was young, he wanted to be a police officer, then a construction worker, then a Bollywood actor, then a farmer, or anything as long as it was off the trains. He said he knew someday, somehow, he would get off the trains. We pray that the outreach to Raju will be successful and someday he will get the help he needs to get off the trains.

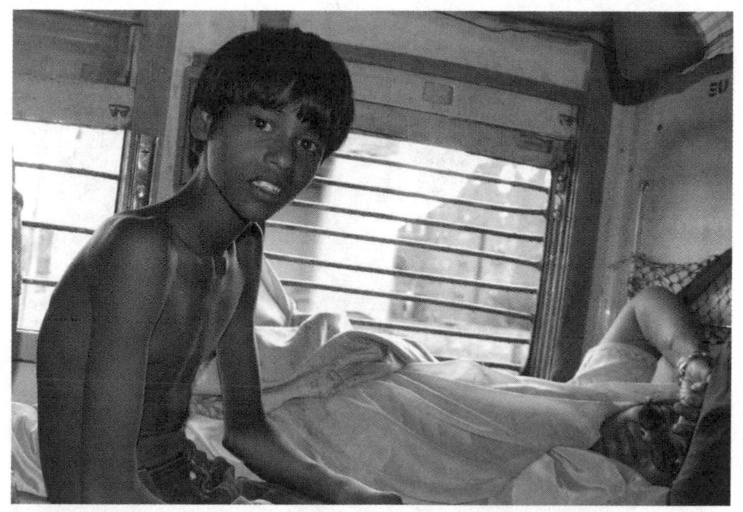

Raju talking with us on the train

Raju picking out shoes

The pastors are helping Raju pick out food for his family

John and a Life Light team member posing with Raju in his new clothes

Lali, Sonali, Aloki and Aunty

Human Trafficking

One of the children at New Beginnings is believed to have been sold into sex trafficking by her mom. In order to prepare to tell her story we wanted to see if we could visit the red light district or meet with any girls being trafficked in India. One of the Life Light pastors in India does outreach to victims of sex trafficking. He asked one of the brothel owners if she would be interested in talking with us and if we could interview a few of her girls. The madam surprised us by agreeing and saying she would come to our location with three of her workers. She had a few stipulations. We could not take pictures and she had to be present when we talked with the girls.

In return, we were to give each of the ladies sewing machines and cloth to make a saree. We said we agreed and would be glad to provide these in exchange for allowing us to talk with them. The girls she agreed to bring were to be her youngest workers. We provided funds for a rickshaw to bring them to our location. They came to visit us after the children had gone to school so it would not be a disruption to them. In preparation, we prayed for God's guidance on how to talk with the Aunty and the girls. We made a call to our home church and solicited advice from our minister, Steve, and his daughter, Carmen. Carmen had been involved in fighting human trafficking, so she gave us sound advice on approaching these girls.

Bruce felt we should ask Aunty if we could interview her first and have the girls have chai in another room while we talked. Our goal was to try to win her trust in order to speak with the girls alone. The time finally came for the girls to arrive. When they walked into the room, Aunty was confident and looked us straight in the eye, while the girls looked down and seemed very nervous. It was clear the three ladies she brought were in their twenties and not in their teens as requested. We made introductions and welcomed Aunty, Aloki, Sonale, and Lali. We asked Aunty if we could speak with her first since she was the boss and then we'd talk to the ladies. She was pleased with that, and wanted to talk and share how she became involved in this business.

Aunty, Age Thirty-nine

Aunty was not shy and was very open about her life. She shared that she was married at the age of thirteen to a man twenty years older than her. She has five children, two daughters, and three sons. Aunty got into this business seventeen years ago, at the age of twenty-two. With her husband drinking away any money he made, she had to try to work to provide for her children. She worked at brickyards and construction sites, also, she sewed and cleaned pots and pans. But, none of this paid enough to feed and education her children. She shared that one day, a lady approached her and promised her money to feed and educate her children, along with a pretty saree to wear. Aunty showed concern about what would happen if her family found out she was in this profession. The lady taught her to leave home every day at the same time and work in a different town, then return home at the same time every night. This way it gives the appearance of going to a regular job each day.

She shared that people may suspect, but they do not know for sure, since one's business is elsewhere. Aunty shared that this lady would give her the money for food, school fees, uniforms, and books for her children, along with clothes for her to wear. Aunty had to work off this debt through her services to the lady's clientele. She shared that the first month she cried constantly, but she did it to keep her children from starving and so they would have a different life than hers. She shared that her sons have all gone to university and are married. Her daughters all went to school and she has arranged good marriages for them in another town. She firmly believes her children have no idea what she does for a living. They believe she runs HIV clinics and programs with the government.

Aunty showed us pictures of her with many prominent India government officials. We think this was done to let us know she had powerful clients. She left working for the other lady seven years ago to start her own business. She shared that there are sixty girls working for her now and that the youngest is seventeen years old. She wanted us to know she looked out for her girls. They were given condoms and HIV education. That she provided them with health care and if any of them got pregnant she had a physician who would provide safe abortions. She personally took her girls to and from their clients to guarantee their safety. For this she took 50 percent of what they made. The fees were 200 rupees for an hour and

1,000 rupees for the full night. (Note: Aloki, Sonale, and Lali agreed there were around sixty girls working for Aunty. They disagreed saying that the youngest girl was thirteen, and that she did provide them with condoms, HIV information, and physician care. They also agreed that her take of their earnings was 50 percent and the fees she shared were correct, but they disagreed that she did not make sure they got to and from calls safely, and they were frequently beaten up by clients).

Aunty is a devoted Muslim. She shares that she does her daily prayers and that only her god will judge if she has done right. Several times during our conversation she asked if we knew a way for her and her girls to get out of this business. She shared that all of the women in her employ would be dead, if not for the work she provided them. They all were in dire circumstances when she found them. The women, and in many cases their children, were close to death from starvation and disease. She shared that she arranges for some of the young women to marry. She likes when a girl gets married and has a stable life. She told us her goal was to give these woman stable lives.

We pushed for ideas on how to get out of this business, and as much as I wanted to be upset with this lady, it was hard. What choices did she really have to support her family? None we discussed provided as well for them based on the fact they were women with no education or skills. Aunty shared, "This business does not give any happiness, never do we get any happiness. I kept my home separate from my life. I corrupted my life, but kept my home safe and secure. It proved very well for my children. Many women in this business also corrupt their children – I did not." As we discussed ways to get out of this business, she challenged us saying, "Tell me of a way for us to make this much money to support our families and we will leave this business now."

Aloki, Age Twenty-seven

Aloki was married at the age of eleven to a twenty-six year old truck driver. She has two children, a girl, fifteen, and a boy, twelve. Both go to school. She hopes they go to college. Aloki is a very beautiful young woman. She tells us that she got into this business when her husband started losing money. He gambles and drinks away his paycheck. She was unable to pay her children's tuition and they were starving. She tried working construction and cleaning pots and pans. One day her son asked her, "Why did you bring me into this world if you could not care for me?" She felt so bad she knew she had to find a way to earn more money. She met Aunty and decided to prostitute herself to focus on her children's future and not hers. Aunty promised she would earn enough to make sure Aloki's children had all they needed for school and food to be healthy. Aunty also promised her pretty new sarees to wear.

Aloki also shared that her family has no clue what she does. She leaves at the same time every day and returns home at the same time every night. When she first started, she shared she cried every time, but now it is easier. She has some constant customers. She meets them in other towns in ditches or fields. Right now, she has ten constant customers a month, which gives her 1,000 rupees a month. She never does any overnight work so she can always be home with her children. She shared one time her husband beat her and accused her of being a prostitute. She did not admit anything to him. She shook her head, laughed and said, "He never complains when I give him money!"

She desires for her children to become engineers or teachers, anything better than her and her husband. When asked what else she could do for a living, she said once her children were done with university, she could do something like scrub pots or construction. But, until her children are through school she will not leave prostitution. We asked if she is ever afraid.

She shared she is afraid of god and that people will give her a bad name, causing her family and children to find out what she does for a living. I asked what god she is afraid of and she shared that she believes that all gods are the same. But, that many people focus on one god. She is Hindu so she believes that there are many gods.

Aloki asked if she could ask us some questions. Her first question was why we like interviewing her and what we thought was nice about her. I told her I liked her beautiful smile, eyes that sparkle, her strength, and her desire and commitment for her children to be educated. She then asked if we could get her children to an American university so they can get away from all of this forever. She asked if we had children and any pictures we could show her of them. We shared their pictures on our cell phone with her. Before Aloki left us, we asked if we could pray for her. She said yes, so we all prayed for Aloki.

Sonale, Age Twenty-nine

Sonale had a strength to her and seemed to be in charge like Aunty. As we talked we learned that Sonale was second in command for the brothel. Her job was to recruit and introduce girls into the business. She was not as open as Aunty and Aloki. She did not want to share much information, and we had to ask her questions in several different ways to get answers. We did learn that she was a Muslim and that thanks to this business her children were all going to a mosque run school. She had six children, four boys, and two girls. She claimed her husband left her for another woman.

She shared that five years ago she was in the hospital for seizures. The doctor told her she needed medicine but she had no funds to pay for her care. In India, you have to pre-pay for your medical care to be given. When the doctor learned of her situation, he told her he knew of a woman who may be able to help her. Help was wanted and Sonale asked to meet the woman. Soon Aunty came to visit her in the hospital. Aunty told her she would pay for her medicine and that she would have to work for her to cover the costs. Aunty told her that this business could provide for her and her children. She promised her pretty sarees to wear too.

Sonale did not share if getting into the business was hard for her. She was strictly business and never smiled while we talked with her. She had a strictness about her. She did talk about getting upset when clients did not pay for their services. She also does not like it when clients beat up the workers. These two things make her very angry. She shared that the business would not be too bad if these things did not happen.

Lali, Age Twenty-five

Aunty, Aloki, and Sonale all were strong and healthy looking woman. Lali on the other hand, did not seem healthy. She was visibly depressed and desperate. She was much thinner than the other ladies and her eyes were tired and sad. She drank her chai and ate the cookies in a way that we knew she was hungry. It took a while for Lali to open up to us. She shared that she was married at the age of eleven to a man forty years older than her. Her parents had six daughters and four sons. They married her off to have one less to feed. Lali told us her husband is now sixty-five and unable to work because he is deaf. It is up to her to support him, their two sons, and herself.

Lali got into this business three years ago. Sonale found her, and her children, starving to death. She provided Sonale with food relief, and in return, expected Lali to provide services to some clients. Lali shared that Sonale promised her that her children would not starve, she would be given funds to send them to school and she would have pretty sarees to wear. Lali shared her first time was horrible and she cried for a month.

She did not do it again for several months, she felt so bad. As she watched her children have very little, if anything to eat, she could not bear to see their hunger and went back to work for Aunty.

Lali said she does not do as much work as the other woman. Just enough to pay for her sons' schooling and to provide food so they don't starve. Lali shared that the food we provided this afternoon was the first food she had today. She makes sure her sons are fed first. She did work as a pot scrubber, but the money she made barely provided a meal a day for her family. Her sons begged and were rag pickers. She has tried other jobs but none have paid enough to support her family.

When we asked Lali what makes her happy. She said, "There is no happiness for me. Too much a difficult life. I cannot die because of my children. If I did not have children I would kill myself. I cannot live because this is such a horrible life. Life of a woman is the worst. The life of a donkey is better than the life of a woman. Please do something to help me." When asked what help she needed. She was quick to respond, if we could help her get some small business that would allow her to survive and get out of this business, she would quit right now.

John told her about New Beginnings Children home. He asked if he got sponsors for her boys to cover their education would she be able to provide for her and her husband with sewing. She said, "Maybe yes." We saw a slight change in her eyes. A glimmer of hope. We told her the boys would be sponsored, but that she must, for their sake, take care of herself. We asked John to tell her that her life has value and that our God says in His word that she is important. We will pray that she learns about our Jesus and how He loves her. During this, Lali was looking directly into my eyes, not at John as he translated.

She responds, "It is a difficult life." I reached out and took Lali's hands, telling her, "There is hope. Even in the hardest places, we must hold on to that hope. It is an honor and a privilege to meet you, Lali."

We then got up as the other ladies had returned to get their saree cloth and sewing machines. Aunty is signaling that she is ready for them to leave. Lali walked around to me, takes my head in her hands, then places her hands on my shoulders, and then kneels with her hands on my feet. John explains that Lali is honoring me. As she stands, I take Lali's head and as Lali says, "No, No, No!", I place my hands on her shoulders and then kneel holding Lali's feet, praying for this precious daughter to know how worthy and loved she is by our Lord and Savior. As I stood up, we see that Lali has finally smiled.

About meeting Aunty, Aloki, Sonali, and Lali

After these ladies had departed, I was emotionally drained. I tried to imagine being in the position of having to choose between watching my children starve or selling my body to care for them. It is hard to understand the pain it must have taken for these ladies to make the choice of the lesser of these two evils. We drilled the pastors on the costs of living and if they could provide for their families on their salaries in construction or cleaning pots. We determined those jobs may provide for minimal daily food such as one, or two, light meals a day. It would not allow for sufficient food, shelter, and education for their children.

We discussed what business could be brought back to these uneducated woman to teach them a skill so they could provide for their families. The best option we could come up with was sewing. We pray that the sewing machines will give an ability to earn a living for their families. The ladies all shared that this was a young woman's business and that one day they would be too old to work. Aunty said in her interview several times that she worries for the women as they get older. What will they be able to do to survive? They hope in their children's educations to be their way out of this life, and that their children will help provide for them as they get older.

We will never forget the stories these ladies shared with us. We pray for Lali, and that the pastors' outreach to her will be successful. Her sons' educations are now covered and they have food support. I will always cherish the smile that Lali showed when our conversation was done and honor was given to this desperate, depressed woman, telling her that she has value and honor. We pray that she will find the hope and future that knowing Jesus will bring.

Meeting these ladies gave us insight into this business and how it works in India. This would help to prepare us for our final story, a story about a precious girl named Priti. Please remember as you prepare to read Priti's story, the points we learned from the ladies. They were all brought into this business by promises of things they greatly desired such as medical care, food, and education for their children. They each were offered pretty sarees to wear. All the ladies confirmed of knowing mothers that had sold their daughters into the business to clear their own debts or make additional funds. They all talked of the abuse they suffered at the hands of their clients. They all were stuck working to pay a debt that would take years to repay.

Heather, Aunty, and John

Aloki talking with us

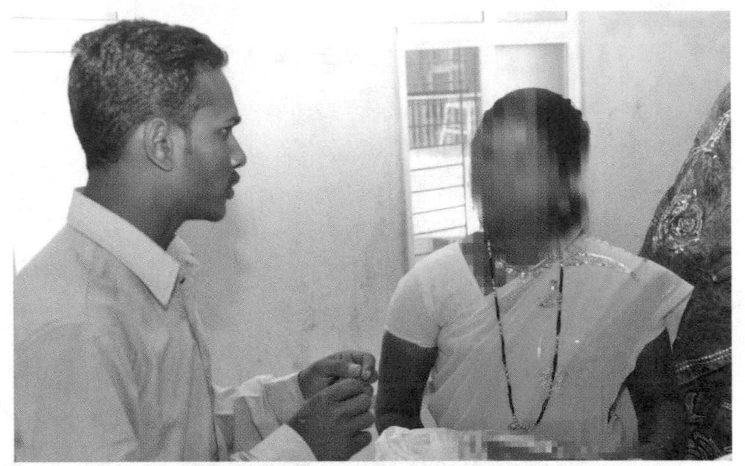

Pastor and Lali talking

Liz and Lali

Priti & Pooja

Age Six

Baba is taking me to live in a children's home that the pastor told him about. He said it will be better for me to live in the children's home. It has been hard for us since Aaie died. He said he can't take care of me. My older brothers and sisters can work to help, but I am too little. In the children's home, he said I will have good food, clothes, and get an education. Baba says he will visit me and I will come home during school breaks. We arrive at New Beginnings Children's Home. There are a lot of boys here and a few girls. I listen as Baba talks to the people who will take care of me here. He tells them my name is Pooja and that I am six years old. They explain that the program at the children's home has just been changed to have girls too. There are four other girls right now. I hear them saying more girls will be added.

I am taken to a room where I will now live. The other girls

are smiling at me. The boys are playing and are very loud. Baba tells me he will see me at break. I cry when he leaves because I don't know anyone here and will miss my family. One of the girls comes up to me and smiles. She tells me that we will be ok. Her name is Priti. I like her name it means "love." She is very pretty and I like her. She and I will share a bunk bed. I have never had a bed before. It is very nice. I tell Priti that my Aaie died and Baba has brought me here to go to school. She says her Aaie left them to live in Mumbai. Her Baba also brought her here to go to school. Her Baba is a construction worker here in town, but it is better for her to live here. She tells me there is more food, fun, and school. We have dahl and rice for dinner. It is good. I go to bed glad that Priti is in the bed right above me. She is my new friend.

Priti and I will both be in Standard One together in school. We have uniforms to wear to school. In the mornings, we get up and make our beds. We then exercise. Once that is done, we get cleaned up and dressed. Our house parents then teach us songs and a lesson from the Bible. We also learn to pray. We eat breakfast and then ride in the school bus to our school. The boys go in one bus and the girls in another bus. I like it at school and do very well in my lessons. When we are not at school, Priti likes to draw and color, and I like to play pots and pans. We also have chores to do which include sweeping and cleaning our room. The house parents show us how to wash our clothes and hang them to dry. Sometimes we also get to help in the kitchen. I like to help in the kitchen. I like living at New Beginnings Children's Home and I am glad to have my friend, Priti.

Age Ten

Priti and I are ready to start Standard Five. She is very smart and gets high marks in her school work. I pass, but am not in as high a position in our class as Priti. In school, Priti likes to study English. I like to study History. Priti reads English poems and copies them into her journal. She also puts her favorite songs and Bible verses in her journal. We like to sing our favorite song together. It goes like this:

Read your Bible,
Pray everyday,
Pray everyday,
Pray everyday.
Read you Bible,
Pray everyday,

And we grow, grow, grow.
And we grow, grow, grow.
And we grow, grow, grow.

There are three rooms of girls now at New Beginnings Children's Home. We have lots of girls to play with, but Priti and I are still best friends. We are the second oldest girls in the home. We get to help take care of the younger girls. We teach them how to help with chores at the home. There is a courtyard and fields at New Beginnings. We have planted flowers, bushes, a vegetable garden, and trees. There is extra construction materials that we can play with outside. We use the bricks and rebar to build little play houses on the ground. We also like to lay the bricks out on the ground in the shape of a house with rooms inside. We fill the rooms with toys, cloth, or other discarded materials that we pretend are furniture and other things we need in a house. There is always something to keep us busy here at the home. I prefer to play outside in the shade. Priti doesn't mind being outside or inside.

Priti tells me that she is worried for her Aaie. Whenever Priti's Aaie comes from Mumbai and visits she has a different uncle with her. Priti told me these men are not really her uncles. She wishes her Aaie would just come and visit her without bringing these men with her. Priti tells me that she wishes Aaie would go back to her Baba. Priti's Baba lives here in town and visits the home some Sundays to see Priti. She loves her Baba, but worries and prays for her Aaie.

Breaks from school are a sad time for me. I am glad to see Baba, but I miss Priti when I am home for break. She goes to stay with her Baba too. We both miss the food, our beds, toys, and even our chores. When we are back home there is not as much to eat and we don't have beds to sleep in. When we get back from break we always talk, and talk, and talk. It is good to be back at New Beginnings Children's Home with Priti, the house parents, and the other kids.

Age Eleven

Priti's Baba came to talk with the house parents today. He is worried for Priti's safety. The house parents come and talk with Priti telling her that she must never go anywhere with her Aaie unless they know about it ahead of time. They explain to Priti that her Aaie has gotten into some bad things and they are worried for Priti's safety. Her Baba and the house parents all warn Priti that she must be careful of her Aaie. Priti comes to me to talk about what they told her. She asks me to pray for her Aaie. She is worried that something is wrong and she is in danger. Priti does not like the men that come to visit with her Aaie and wonders if one of them is the trouble. I tell her we will pray. I tell her that she can talk to her Aaie about her worries when she comes for Priti's birthday.

It is Priti's twelfth birthday today. Priti is excited because her Aaie always comes for her birthday. Priti tells me she hopes her Aaie comes alone. What Priti wants most of all is to spend time alone with her Aaie. I see a car pull up the driveway and from the window I can tell her Aaie is not alone this time. I feel bad for Priti and know she will be disappointed. The same man from last year has come with Priti's Aaie. He is introduced again as her uncle to the house parents. Priti's Aaie has brought a cake and we each get a small piece to eat.

Priti shortly after arriving to live at New Beginnings Children's Home

I notice this "uncle" is looking at all of us girls. I don't like the way he looks at me with no smile. He just stares at us very carefully. The house parents do not leave the entire time Priti's Aaie visits. Finally, she and "uncle" leave. Priti is sad that she did not get to spend time alone with her Aaie. Priti is always smiling and never gets mad. It makes me sad to see her sad like this over her Aaie's visit.

A few months after Priti's birthday we are working in the garden when we see a man walking by himself up the side of the yard fence and along the back of the home. We see our security man going to check on what the man is doing. We all stop working to watch the security man get to the other man. He and the man talk for a while and then the man quickly leaves. I think the man looks familiar. A little later, Priti is called to the house parents. They want to talk with her. She comes back and tells me that the man we saw was the man her Aaie makes her call uncle. Her Aaie was not with him and the house parents are concerned he was up to no good. They asked her if she had seen or heard from her Aaie. Priti has not heard from Aaie and does not know what that man was doing walking the home boundaries.

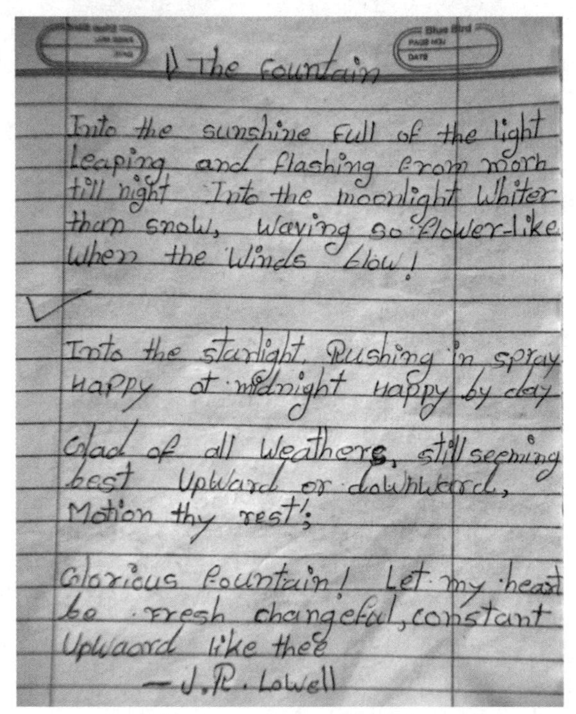

1) The fountain

Into the sunshine Full of the light
Leaping and flashing From morn
till night Into the moonlight Whiter
than snow, Waving so flower-like
When the Winds blow!

Into the starlight Rushing in spray
Happy at midnight Happy by day
Glad of all Weathers, still seeming
best Upward or downward,
Motion thy rest;

Glorious fountain! Let my heart
be fresh changeful, constant
Upward like thee
— J.R. Lowell

English poem written in Priti's journal

Age Thirteen

Priti and I are in Standard Seven now at the government run school that the children at New Beginnings Children's Home attend. Priti's English is very good and she gets all A's in her English class. She showed me a very long poem written in English that she likes so much that she wrote it down in her journal. I am happy that we're best friends and share our journals with each other. Priti also draws beautiful designs in her journals. We hung a picture of a giraffe she drew to decorate our wall in our bedroom by our bunk beds. Priti is so smart and can do so many creative things. She helps me with my Math and English homework. School is much harder now and we spend time studying every day.

Today is Assembly Day at school and there is much excitement. Priti shows me the watch her Baba gave her has stopped working. We are in a hurry to get to school so I tell her we will look at it on our way. In the school bus, she keeps tapping her watch to try to make it work again. Sadly, we cannot make her watch work again. I tell her that it is still a nice gift from her Baba.

When we get to school, we all visit outside until it is time to go to our homeroom. Many of the girls have beautiful sarees on for the assembly today. As Priti and I are visiting, one of the older girls calls that Priti's Aaie is over at the side of the school and wants to see her.

Priti and I go over to the side of the school and her Aaie is across the street wanting to see her. Priti and I walk over. She tells Priti that she was passing through town and thought she would stop by the school to spend some time with her. Priti tells her that it is Assembly Day at school and hopes she could see her later on. Priti's Aaie says that she only has time to spend with her right now and she thinks it would be nice if they went together to get her a beautiful new saree for her upcoming birthday in a few days. She shares that she will not be able to come back for a while. Priti looks unsure about going and asks if I could come with them. Priti's Aaie says, "No, that is not a good idea, I don't want to make Pooja late for school." Priti hesitates, and her Aaie looks hurt and says, "Don't you want to spend time alone with me? Just you and me?" Priti smiles a huge smile and says, "Yes!" Priti tells me to go back to school and that her Aaie would bring her back to school in a little bit.

Priti and Pooja

Priti showing her new bed

I watched them walk away and turn a corner. I thought about how much it meant to Priti to spend some time alone with her Aaie. I also thought about the house parents saying it was unsafe for Priti to go with her Aaie without them knowing about the visit. I decided to hurry into school and tell our homeroom teacher. The teacher immediately called New Beginnings to let the house parents know that Priti had gone off from school with her Aaie.

I went to the assembly and kept watching for Priti to come back. Finally, one of the house parents got me out of class to ask me exactly what I saw. I told him the whole story. He was very worried and upset for Priti. He was making phone calls while we talked. I heard him saying that they watched all the ways out of town and checked the whole town but there was no sign of Priti anywhere. He told the pastor that he thought Priti's Aaie took her out of town before he was notified that she had been taken, that there must have been a car waiting that ran them straight out of town. I felt afraid and helpless for my best friend and started praying for her right away.

It is not the same at New Beginnings Children's Home without my best friend. I look at her picture and read her journal all the time. It helps keep her with me. I pray that wherever she is that she is safe. I heard that one of the house parents got a call from a Mumbai number and when he answered the call, the phone hung up immediately. He tried calling and calling the number back hoping it was Priti trying to reach out to us. A few days later when he tried the phone number again it was disconnected. Priti, like all of us kids, know the house parents' cell phone numbers. If she was able, I know she would call to let us know she was safe. She would not let us worry like this for her. I also remember how she told me her Aaie did bad things and was a prostitute. This makes me think something bad has happened to her – something very bad.

Priti at a Valentine's Day celebration

Priti and friends at New Beginnings Children's Home

About meeting Priti

We did not have the opportunity to meet Priti, but she is the reason we went to India. We wanted to give her a voice and share her story. In order to do this, we looked through Priti's belongings that were left at the home when she was abducted. Her journals, drawings, and favorite Bible verses and songs. We interviewed her closest friends at the home in a group forum. Pooja led most of the discussion as her best friend and the friend who was with her when she left with her mother.

We also talked with the house parents at New Beginnings about their search for Priti. They were clearly upset that Priti was taken. They told us how Priti's mother always came with a different man that she would introduce as Priti's uncle when she visited. They also shared that during the last two visits the same man came with her and that same man was found a few months after she visited checking the boundaries of the children's home. They believe that he found that the children's home was too secure of a place to abduct Priti and set up the abduction at the school. The house parents shared how they warned Priti to not go off alone with her mother and to let them know of all contact she had with her mother. After speaking with Priti's father, they knew he was concerned that the mother would try to sell her daughter into prostitution. They shared how as soon as the school called, they put out an alarm sending people to all the paths out of town to block them from leaving. She was not found in any of the markets, at the airport, train station, or in a car exiting the main roads from the town. It is thought a car was waiting that rushed them straight out of town.

The house father who got the hang up call from Mumbai shared with tears in his eyes how he called and called that number hoping it was Priti, and she would find a way to answer to tell them where she was taken. Also, that a few days later the number was disconnected. He told us how Priti's father and he went to the police to try to get help. The police's stance was a mother has the right to take her child. They would not provide any assistance.

When we asked her friends what they thought happened to Priti, they each thought her mother sold her into prostitution. They were all positive that is what happened from what Priti had told them about her mother. Pooja said she thought Priti's mother had sold her and sent her out of the country, otherwise she knew Priti would call. It broke our hearts when Pooja looked trustingly at us and asked us to please help bring her friend back. We told her we would do our best to share Priti's story, but we did not know if it would bring her back. Bruce asked the girls if any of them were worried that what happened to Priti would happen to them. It was sad that three of the four girls were concerned that their parents or relatives might sell them for money.

Human trafficking is a major issue in India. According to a Fox News article by Brent Martz, published on July 22, 2013, titled, "Human Trafficking will not end until it ends in India":

> *India is the epicenter of human trafficking-including 100 million people with 1.2 million child prostitutes. It tops the list of countries when it comes to transit, destination and source of human trafficking victims. According to the United Nations, the most dangerous place in the world to be a girl or woman is India.*

We wish we could say this is an isolated incident, but, as the article goes on to say, "Two hundred thousand Indian children a year are sold into slavery, many by their parents for a mere $17 dollars."

Priti with some friends

Priti showing a flower in the garden

From the time we heard of Priti's story at the International Conference of Missions, we wanted to share it. We pray she is somehow safe and that the songs and Bible verses she learned at New Beginnings are bringing her hope and comfort in her current situation. We know Jesus is with this precious child.

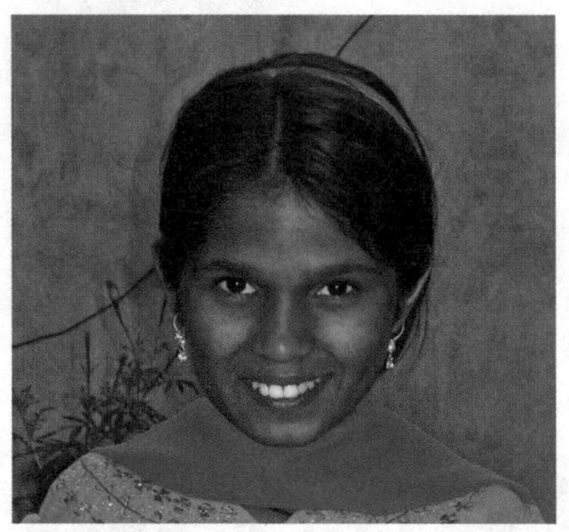

Most recent picture available of Priti

Date of Birth: January 25, 1998
Missing Date: January 19, 2011

If you have seen this child, please notify Life Light (contact information at the end of this book) or the authorities immediately.

Life Light Team

Bruce and I are sincerely grateful for the time and assistance that were provided to us by the Life Light team. Their knowledge, talents, and dedication were a blessing to us, just as much as they must be to the children in New Beginnings Children's Home – and to the community in which they serve. It was a blessing to spend time with these servants of the Lord. The outreach services that they administer in India seemed both exciting and overwhelming to us. The sheer volume of the tremendous daily need would overwhelm even the best of us. Yet, everyday this team of missionaries, pastors, and house parents take care of what they can – one person or child at a time. They are able to focus on and handle what is in front of them. Due to the sensitivity of the country, and Christian persecution, we will not share the actual names of the team in India and locations where they work.

Papa and children

English school run by Life Light

The founder of Life Light Mission is the father of two of the missionaries on the team. We will call him Papa as do all the children they serve at New Beginnings Children's Home. Papa shared with us that he grew up in a Christian home for boys, and twenty years ago he started this home to help children in

India. Life Light also runs an English school which is government recognized but non-aided. It serves over four hundred kids from the ages of four to sixteen. The school offers classes from nursery through Standard Seven. The school gives Life Light the opportunity to reach out to those in the community and show them Christ's unconditional love. Students are taught God's love through Bible study. They also celebrate Christian holidays to further educate the children. While we were working with Life Light, we were offered the opportunity to visit the English school. We spent time in several of the classrooms getting to know the children and letting them ask us questions. They asked us to sing our national anthem and then to sing our favorite Christian song. After singing, *The Star-Spangled Banner*, we finished our singing debut with, *Awesome God*. There was polite applause but no further requests for singing. It was nice to see the Bible being taught in an unreached country to Hindu, Muslim, and the Christian children. We pray that the values and Word being taught will bring this generation to know the Lord and Savior – Jesus!

Life Light has a staff of pastors that work with all of the different services that Life Light has in India. These pastors work amongst the poorest people in the world. They go to the slums throughout their area for outreach. They go to the brick factories, the brothels, gypsy camps, and leper colonies – wherever God leads them to serve. They took us to a gypsy camp of sugarcane harvesters to see how they work and live. It was clear the pastor had strong, amicable relationships with the people working in the fields. We sat with the field workers in their camp drinking tea that they made fresh for us using the sugarcane they had just harvested. It was the best cup of tea we had ever tasted.

Life Light took us along to help serve a meal to a local leper colony. Life Light provides food, hope, and encouragement to these people infected with leprosy. The lepers shared with us that there were over 1,000 men, women, and children living in this leper colony. It was very upsetting to see the conditions in which these people live. They are forced to live away from society and are shunned from being able to get jobs. One person shared with us they were sent away from their family when they contracted the disease. Another shared they had just come from begging at the temple. That is how they try to survive, along with rag picking.

That day we watched the Life Light staff as they served a meal to a group of lepers from the colony. We asked why we could not take the meal into the colony and were told it would incite a riot. So, the pastors brought plastic bags and all the leftover food was bagged up for the lepers at the meal to take back and share with the rest of the leper colony. The people ate the food as if they were starving. They had missing limbs, sores, and skin issues. The older ones looked so very tired. We had no idea leprosy still existed. According to the World Health Organization (http://www.who.int/en/), India accounts for 58 percent of the newly diagnosed leprosy cases in the world. This is a disease that can be cured with medicine. One of the pastors shared that the medicine is expensive and has to be taken for six months, to up to a year, depending on the type of leprosy. The people in the colony did not have the funds for the medicine and there was minimal help from the government to provide treatment.

Life Light staff at the English school offer church services on Sunday. We were pleased to see some of the students attending church. In India, the women and men tend to sit on separate sides of the church with the children sitting in front. Church service is very lively, full of music and teaching. Communion is served every Sunday. Considering baptism is a serious decision for followers of Jesus, in some areas in India, they have to register with the court as Christians and proclaim they have made this decision freely. Several people we interviewed said they accepted Jesus as their Lord and Savior but were not yet baptized due to fear of their families not accepting them once they converted. These pastors work under the risk of persecution. Even with the risk, we saw these brave pastors boldly proclaim Jesus wherever they went. We watched one pastor openly sharing the gospel in the middle of a train full of Sikh worshipers. His devotion to openly sharing the gospel was inspiring to us.

People from the leper colony waiting to eat

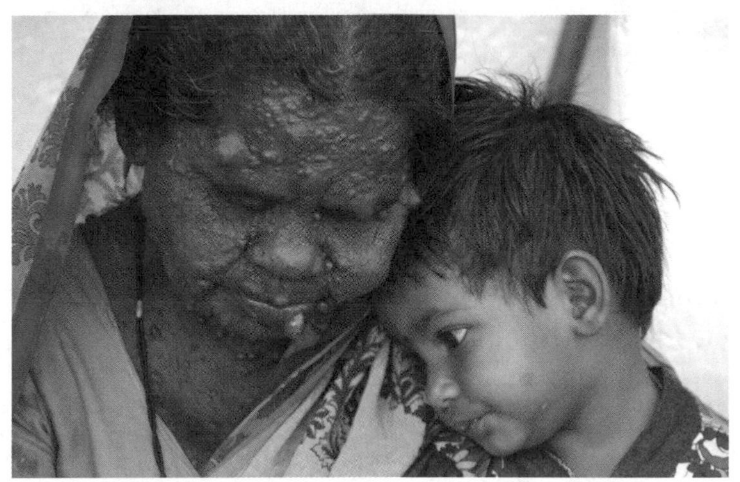

Grandmother and granddaughter from the leper colony

The pastors are very involved in New Beginnings Children's Home. They help to identify and bring children who need assistance to the home. The pastors assist in interviewing and selecting the best Christian house parents to work and live at the children's home too. The house parents are amazing in the way they care for eighty-four children every day and make it appear effortless. After the children completed their 5:00 a.m. calisthenics, made their beds, got cleaned up, and dressed for the day, the house parents would take turns leading the children in worship songs and teaching a lesson from the Bible. Soon after this, the children would eat breakfast and perform light chores before the school buses would come. Once the children were off to school, the home staff would all attend devotion time. We joined them in singing worship songs and reading a devotion together.

The house parents took great care of the children. At times, we found the volume of children overwhelming. However, we never heard a house parent raise a voice. They calmly instructed the children with loving direction. They checked that the children were clean, well fed, that chores were being done, took care of the occasional dispute, helped with homework, and taught them about Jesus. These children had songs memorized, and not just Bible verses, but whole chapters of the Bible memorized. They loved to recite chapters of the Bible to us and they seemed to favor the Psalms.

With all this work to oversee the children, the house parents could be found playing with the children out in the yard, dancing with the girls or playing cricket with the boys, and sitting and talking with the teenagers. They take care of small hurts when the little ones fall down and need extra attention, and they seem to have endless energy and patience.

Church services – women and men sit on different sides of the church

House father seeing the kids off to school

Church services are also performed at New Beginnings Children's Home. It was wonderful to see eighty-four children, in India, lifting up their voices to Jesus; and even more so, to see these children sitting perfectly still listening to the message. We were asked to preach on one Sunday to the children at New Beginnings. We decided to have some of the kids help with the message. The older girls were taught the song, *Awesome God*, to perform during worship. The boys acted out the anointing of King David.

One of the house fathers performed as Jesse, and Bruce as Samuel. The children had never seen a Bible account acted out and were poised with attention. The actors were very dramatic and the lesson meaningful. We told the children that God saw David's heart, and He knew their hearts too. We believed that God had selected and anointed each of them through bringing them to this home for a purpose. The children enjoyed the lesson and many said that they wanted to act out another Bible story.

We are excited to share that two of the girls we interviewed in India just turned eighteen and were baptized. These children that the Life Light staff are raising at New Beginnings Children's Home are the future of India and will have the job of helping to bring Jesus to this unreached nation.

Kitchen staff and children do all the cooking over wood fires

House father leading the daily staff devotion

House mother leading children in worship

House parents with children

House father leading worship

House mother playing "Hey Girl"

House mother with girls

Sunset at New Beginnings Children's Home

What Can We Do?

Even though we knew India was going to be a tough trip for us from what we had studied, nothing prepared us for hearing the stories first hand. Stories of female children that were unwanted, children trafficked into bonded labor, sex trafficking, young girls married against their will, children, women, and men tortured and murdered. These children were so brave in telling us their stories.

While we are on the mission field, we do a daily blog to keep our supporters updated on our progress. We wanted to share our final blog from the India trip with you:

To say our hearts are broken for the people of India is all we can say right now to describe how we are feeling. Several people have asked us why we are so sad returning from this trip to India compared to when we came home from St. Vincent, Haiti, and Kenya. On those trips we returned excited and on fire.

The difference is really simple. In St. Vincent, Haiti, and Kenya the church is strong and actively growing. Although poor, the hope found in Jesus is evident everywhere you go in these countries. You know the people there, although in extremely poor conditions, have hope and will be rewarded in eternity.

In India less than 2 percent of the people are Christians. We traveled everywhere seeing the Hindu false idols, Muslim mosques, and Buddhist temples where the people worship. We entered into these places and saw the worship first hand. As we left one Hindu temple for the god Shiva, Bruce shared he felt such a heaviness and oppressing feeling as he walked through this temple.

The hope found in Jesus simply was not there except when we were in the missions with which we worked. It is depressing to know the masses here face an eternity separated from God and a life where the love and grace found in a relationship with Jesus is missing.

Please pray for the people of India and the precious children who face hardships that are still bringing us to tears as we try to process what we have seen, heard, and learned while working in India.

We remain heartbroken for the precious children of India. Now we ask you to please help the children in India. Give prayer. Pray for the children. Pray for the missionaries and pastors in the field working for Life Light. Pray for funding to expand and support the missions' efforts.

Give time. Go and meet with the missions, either in India, or with U.S. team members. Share these stories and the missions' work with your church, family, and friends. Lead fundraising drives to gather much needed supplies or funds for children home expansions, pastor support, Christian schools, or community outreach.

Consider yourself blessed for who you are, where you live, and the many resources you have been given. Please share the resources God has given you. These children have so much to offer, and with our support, they will thrive and grow up to bring positive changes for the next generation in India. Be a part of helping Christianity thrive and grow in this unreached nation.

We walked in on the boys laying hands on and praying for this sick boy

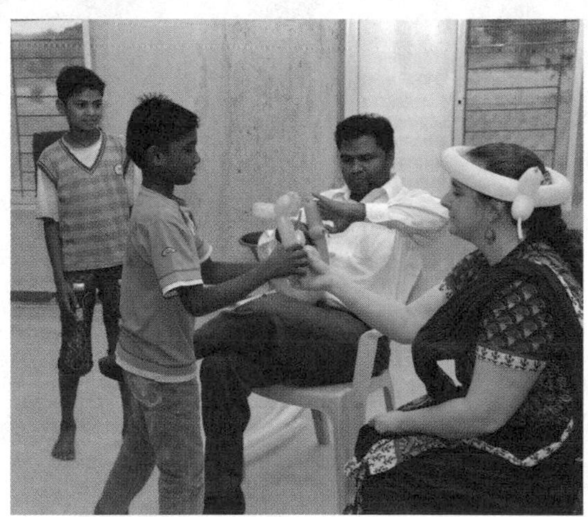

John and Heather making balloon animals for the children

Bruce and Heather riding in the ox cart at the sugarcane camp

Heather and Liz tasting sugarcane

Bruce and Liz having lunch with the Life Light pastors and staff

The sugar cane camp workers with the Life Light staff, John, Heather, and Liz

Life Light pastors with Aman's family, Heather, Bruce, Liz, and Aman. At the brickyard where Aman lives and works.

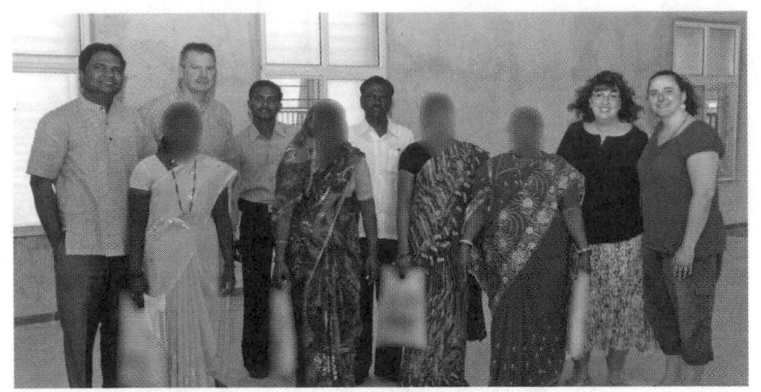

Lali, Sonali, Aloki, Aunty, John, Bruce, Life Light Pastors, Liz, and Heather

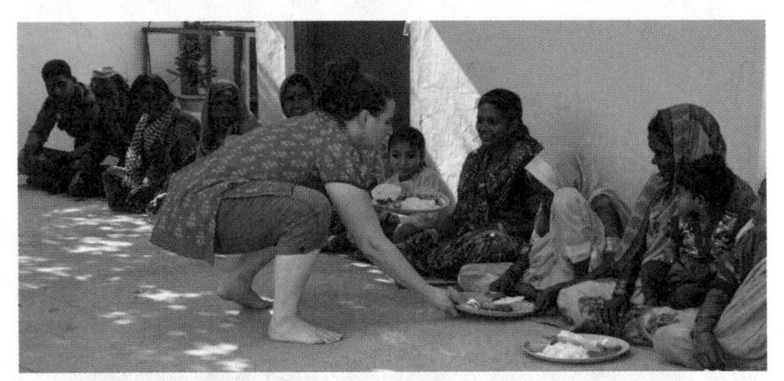

Heather serving food to the ladies from the leper colony

Drawing a picture for us to bring home

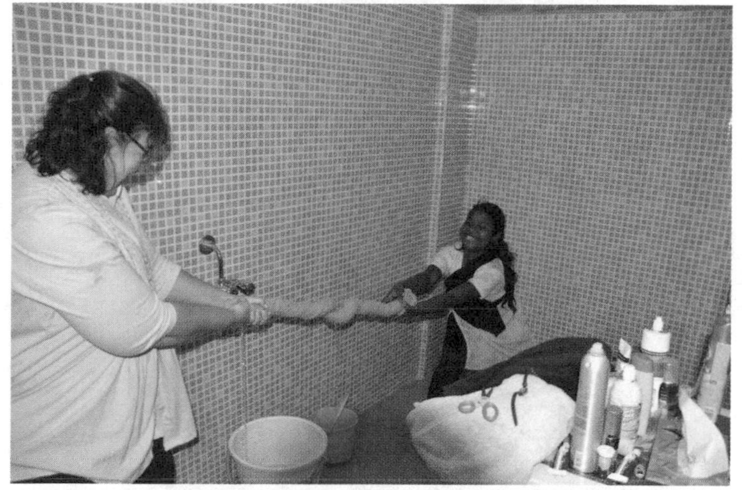

Liz learning how to do laundry by hand

Girls playing a game at New Beginnings Children's Home

Heather spent months knitting hats for all of the children at the home

Everyone got a hat!

The children being treated to a Chicken Biryani dinner.

Heather helping make bracelets

Leena and Liz showing the bracelets they made for each other

Bruce watching Leena make mud pies

Bruce with boys following him through the children's home

Kishan giving Liz a hug

Liz with the girls at New Beginnings Children's Home

House parents at New Beginnings Children's Home

Teen girls at New Beginnings Children's Home

Boys praying during church service

Girls praying during church service

Support for the Missions Featured in Precious Children of India

To contact or support Life Light of India:

Website: www.lifelightindia.weebly.com
Email: LifeLightIndia@gmail.com

Mail:
Life Light
2850 W. County Road 6
Tiffin, OH 44883

All names of Life Light personnel and the children have been changed to protect their identities. Only the U.S. representatives, John and Heather, will be named by their first names.

About the Author

Elizabeth Carpenter, and her husband, Bruce, have been deeply touched by the desperate needs of children around the world. They answered God's call to give these children a voice by gathering and sharing their stories. From this calling, *His Precious Children: A Story-Sharing Ministry* was formed. Their ongoing passion is to work with needy children around the world and empower them through sharing their stories. Their most recent trip was to India.

Elizabeth and Bruce live in Columbus, Ohio, with their two dogs, Tippy and Zoey. They have two grown children, their daughter, Christina (husband Brian), and son, Zachary; also, like a son, Liz's youngest brother, Kevin. They love being grandparents to Ethan and Oliver too. They are part of the church family at Discover Christian Church in Dublin, Ohio.

Connect with Elizabeth:
www.hispreciouschildren.org
www.facebook.com/hispreciouschildren:

www.hispreciouschildren.org

जिला विधिक सेवा प्राधिकरण, सवाई माधो
हर नागरिक का रक्षक
SAVE the Girl Child
A baby is God's opinion
that life should go on.
बेटी है कुदरत का उपहार
जीने का उसको भी अधिकार
अपनी लाडली को बालिका वधू न बनाए
18की उम्र के बाद ही बिटिया का ब्याह रचायें
जिला विधिक सेवा प्राधिकरण, सवाई माधोपुर द्वारा जनहित में प्रसारित

For 25 years, American Caribbean Experience has been serving the people of Jamaica through education, health care, enterprise and discipleship. From teaching children to read, to pulling teeth, to financing small businesses, to training the island's future chefs and teachers, ACE has taken every measure necessary to "love their neighbors." While this is a story about a particular place and its people, it's also a story about all of us: How God works through broken people and in broken places to do beautiful things.

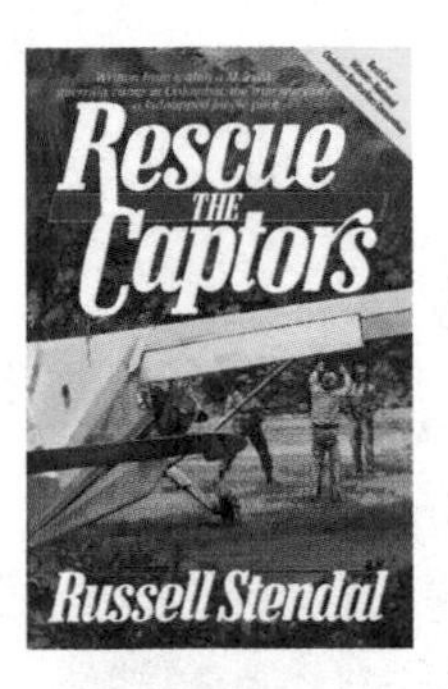

American bush pilot Russell Stendal, on routine business, landed his plane in a remote Colombian village. Gunfire exploded throughout the town, and within minutes Russell's 142-day ordeal had begun. The Colombian cartel explained that this was a kidnapping for ransom and that he would be held until payment was made.

Held at gunpoint deep in the jungle and with little else to occupy his time, Russell got ahold of some paper and began to write. He told the story of his life and kept a record of his experience in the guerrilla camp. His "book" became a bridge to the men who held him hostage and now serves as the basis for this incredible true story of how God's love penetrated a physical and ideological jungle.